# Solomon in All
# His Glory

# Solomon in All His Glory

By

## Robert Lynd

*Essay Index Reprint Series*

**BOOKS FOR LIBRARIES PRESS**
FREEPORT, NEW YORK

First Published 1923
Reprinted 1969

STANDARD BOOK NUMBER:
8369-1420-1


LIBRARY OF CONGRESS CATALOG CARD NUMBER:
72-86769


PRINTED IN THE UNITED STATES OF AMERICA

To
**SYLVIA LYND**

# CONTENTS

viii

# Contents

# SOLOMON IN ALL HIS GLORY

# Solomon in All His Glory

## I

### SOLOMON IN ALL HIS GLORY

NOT to have seen a kingfisher leaves the world
full of a mysterious beauty.  There is still something to be sought for—something prettier than
the North Pole, before it was discovered, and
less impossible as an object of search than
the Holy Grail.  Every river bank along which
one wanders is rich with its unseen colours.
Not a willow grows aslant a brook but might
be the perch of this winged rainbow.  Hence,
I was not melancholy that I had never seen
a kingfisher save in a glass case.  I felt that I
was saving it up—that it decorated to-morrow,
and that to-day, meanwhile, was pleasant enough
with other things.  When I heard, however, that
a kingfisher had come to live within two hundred
yards of me I am not a boor that I could remain
indifferent.  A visitor mentioned casually that he

3

had seen it.  He had seen in a few hours what I
had been looking for for years.  I went out in
the evening with him past the mill, past the duck-
pond with its barbed wire, through a chained
gate into a field, and along the bank of a little
muddy stream overgrown with duckweed and
white crowfoot.  All the birds of the country-side
seemed to be congregated here in search of mois-
ture.  Martins swept down in scores over the face
of the brook, chattering like bathing girls and
gathering up insects on their flight.  Some of
them would rest every now and then on telegraph
wires that crossed the field, carefully preening
every feather, a family party preparing to move.
They will soon, we may take it, be making in a
mob for Africa, though it is less than a fortnight
since I saw the heads of their latest brood gaping
anxiously out of the nests under the eaves and
opening their orange gullets to the parents who
brought food in response to their clamour.  One
remembers that in one's childhood there were
two excitements of summer—the excitement of
going to the seaside and the excitement of going
home.  Similarly, among the birds, there seems
to be an excitement of autumn that responds to
the excitement of spring.  The spotted fly-
catchers, indeed—ridiculously named, for there
are no spots that the naked eye can see—are

rioting in the hedges as they never rioted in
spring. They perch in the thorn bushes over the
river, sylphs of the air and models of silence.
Then, at sight of a fly, comes the dive as from a
spring-board. They can leap upward like a
flame or outward like an arrow. They have all
the graces and the tricks of acrobats. You
seldom see the fly they are after, but their course
is as clever as though the Wandering Rocks were
threatening their tails in vain. Each of them
after its flight returns to its perch to meditate,
casting its wise, grandmotherly eyes down its
slender beak and sitting so still that no insect
could doubt its innocence. More beautiful are
the grey wagtails—also ridiculously named, for
it is their yellow that strikes the eye—that haunt
the hedges of the stream, with tails that seem to
pant with their heart-beats. This is one of the
most beautiful of English birds—beautiful in
colour and beautiful in flight. As it flies, its long
tail gives it something of the grace of the magpie.
Its tail both hampers it and adds to our admiration. It is as though we were watching a beautiful creature performing on the tight rope. Its
flight, as it climbs into the air and at each step
folds its wings, is part of an exquisite ballet.

Yet there is little music to accompany it. The
wren, brown as a withering leaf, pauses and re-

attempts the ancient vehemence of its song as it
hops among the lower branches of the confused
hedge of thorn, sloe and bramble.  But for the
most part it is content to chatter—to scold no
one in particular with its grating churr but the
universe or the young moon.  The robins are
more generous, and recognise that there are other
themes for song than love.  That, I think, is
what has endeared the robin to man. Most of the
other birds are amorists in their music.  The
robins declare that life is good even after the
honeymoon, and that there are twelve months in
the year, all of them good.  They are birds with
all the human vices—greedy, quarrelsome and
domineering—but at least they sing songs of
experience that echo our own—songs in which
joy and sorrow, memory and hope, are inter-
mingled beyond extrication.  Theirs, indeed, is
the only certain music at this season.  You would
not call the noise that the nuthatches make, in-
visibly clicking like typewriters along the
branches of the tall elms, music.  You would not
call the hysterical whinny of the green woodpecker, as he escapes from one patch of trees to
another, music.  Here, but for the robin, is the
silence and the songlessness of autumn.  The
linnets' voices, as they break out of the thorn
and escape into the wide air, are hardly more

than laboured breathing.   The willow-wren and
the white-throat scour the hearts of the bushes
for their insect prey in the timid silence of mice.
All is still as the surface of the dull stream.   The
caw of a rook half-a-mile away would disturb the
silence.

In order to see birds it is necessary to become
a part of the silence.   One has to sit still like a
mystic and wait.   One soon learns that fussing,
instead of achieving things, merely prevents
things from happening.   To be passive is in some
circumstances the most efficient form of activity.
You cannot command events: you can only put
yourself in the place where events will happen
to you.   No impatient man has ever seen Nature.
It is no use bustling after a kingfisher.   I knew
this and, though I have no great taste for
patience, I sat down on the bank of the stream,
idly watching flycatcher and wagtail, the yellow
fleabane, the mauve peppermint, and the fresh
green of the iris leaves.   I did not hope for too
much.   I was content to lie at the edge of a
stream that a kingfisher inhabited.   The unseen
kingfisher made the mud of the stream as pretty
as though it were sitting there on a bough as in
an illustration.   So at least I thought, and I knew
that I was going to return again and again to
the shores of that stagnant streamlet until I

had set my eyes on Solomon in all his glory or whatever a kingfisher most resembled. Then, suddenly, out of a turn of the stream under a thicket of bushes, the blue flame appeared and fled past me along the water, perching for a moment on the lower branch of a willow and taking to flight again as soon as it saw the cat-like eyes of a human being watching it from a few yards' distance. Was I disappointed in the spectacle? No. I am disappointed only because I am unable to describe it. Can you imagine a blue that is more beautiful than any green, and a green that is more beautiful than any blue, and both of them blended as though into a magical light? Perhaps there are waters of as wonderful a blue lying about the shores of some undiscovered island. Perhaps there are waters of as wonderful a green visting the white caves on the shore of that island.

There is surely no other bird that provides us in the same degree with an Arabian afternoon's entertainment. Even in the swiftness with which it melts from the view, it seems to be a piece of a story-teller's world, a visionary figment. The mere gleam of its flashing feathers, when it is past, transforms the muddiest waters into a stream of legend. To have seen it gives one the vanity of a larger experience. But one

is not content. One must see it again—see it in
such a way that the eye can seize it in shape and
in detail and not as a mere fugitive splendour.
One returns the next evening again and lies down
above the fleabane and the peppermint. After a
time a shadow perches under the shadow of an
arch of bushes—takes up its stand on a pole in
mid-stream, like Patience on a monument, and
meditates on minnows. There are no colours to
be seen: it might as well, save for its size, be a
cormorant or the devil. Nor does it wait to be
seen through the field-glasses. Two lovers pass,
and the pole is birdless. I had almost given up
hope of seeing it again when a shape appeared
above the hedge and a little beyond it—a shape
that rose into the light of the sunset and reflected
it in an orange glow, like a winged goldfish. As
it passed, the orange of the underparts melted
into the green and blue of the upper, and it
disappeared, a tiny comet of orange and green,
lovely (said I to myself) as the unity of Ireland.
It is possible that the kingfisher has no politics,
but in legend at least it has always been the
bird of peace. Is it not the halcyon for whose
ark-like nest the waters of the sea were calm?
The ark-like nest, they say, is romance, and the
real nest is but a mess of old bones at the end
of a hole. Humanity was surely justified in pro-

viding it with a house better suited to its fine
robes—in giving this legend among birds a
legendary setting.  It was the only point, indeed,
on which humanity was kind to the kingfisher.
Its fine feathers have brought it not honour, but
persecution—or, perhaps it would be more accurate to say, the honour of persecution.  Yet
it seems reasonable to believe that the world
would be poorer if no one could ever see, or hope
to see, a kingfisher, just as it would be poorer if
no one could ever see a rainbow.  It may be that
there would be no more rainbows if the milliners
could get hold of them and persuade women to
wear them.  Luckily, men have begun to see
that it is necessary to defend the graces of life
against the demands of millinery, and there is a
chance that the kingfisher may survive to amuse
us, as the whirling colours of a humming-top
amuse children.

Many sorts of birds, indeed, have already begun to be more plentiful since it has become less
of a fashion to possess them, living or dead.  If
there are fewer swallows, on account of the
slaughter on their passage through France, there
are more goldfinches.  The birds, however, have
not yet learned to trust man, as you may see
by the behaviour of the green woodpecker, who
fills the wood with mocking noises, but who will

not trust himself within range of a human eye
if he can help it. As I lay among the heather
and gorse on the top of a hill on Sunday a green
woodpecker flew over my head, with a yellow
flash of tail, and dropped with a scream to the
stem of a hawthorne-tree a few yards away. He
clung to it, as if listening, and the sun gleamed
on his green cloak and on the ruby in his crown.
But he no sooner saw me than he screamed again
and fled behind a thicket, beautiful in his un-
gainliness. The hill was also full of redstarts in
their Joseph's coats, flying from covert to covert,
and showing little of their beauty but the tail,
that seemed to be on fire as they disappeared.
They were, for the most part, but a melancholy
voice crying "Coo-ee" behind the leaves. Occasionally, however, cock and hen would settle on
the tips of the branches and carry on their dia-
logue of alarm, he blue, black and red, exquisite
as a Japanese painting, she more domestic in
her brown dress. But at the slightest movement
of one's head they became aware of the presence
of man, the enemy, and were once more crying
fugitives with tails of fire. Here, too, there is
no way to see the world but by sitting still. On
these terms alone will the procession of bright
things go by. If you want an excuse for doing
nothing, here is one ready to your hand.

## II

## CHANGING HOUSES

THERE is much to be said for moving in winter. If you like the house you are leaving, it is best of all to choose a week that would make Paradise itself look dismal. There should be cold without sunshine, a cold wind the colour of dirty water— a wind that withers and benumbs to a point at which you cease to notice or to care whether it is wet or dry. But even ordinary wet weather is better than no bad weather at all. The rain makes you nervous for the piano and the other precious things that are left standing on the road till the men feel strong enough to hoist them into the vans. But better a wet piano than a sad heart. Luckily, the longer the piano is left standing in the rain, the more desperate becomes your impatience to leave the place and to cast off its mud from your boots for ever.

Not that I was ever the sort of person to fall in love with a house in the best of circumstances.

I like places, and I like people, but neither the outside nor the inside of any house matters enough to me to cause me an ache at leaving. I had rather have a house with a view than a house that is itself a view. Mr. Lucas, or some-one else, has said that it is not the house in which one lives, but the house opposite the house in which one lives, that matters. There are, I admit, houses so ugly, so ostentatiously ugly, that I should be reluctant to live in them. Some of them were built at a time when there was rivalry as to who should invent a brick of the most repulsive colour, and one man invented a brick of soapy yellow and another a brick of contusion blue. Every time you look at the front of one of these houses, you feel that the sun has gone out. There is nothing that can bring the cheerfulness of life into their long and dismal faces, from the sharp-angled attic-window down to the bay-windows below, chill with a Miss Murdstoneish self-satisfaction. Were house-fronts designed in imitation of tombstones, you could scarcely get a more depressing effect. There is nothing that persuades one more strongly that civilisation has come to stay than the fact that it survived, not only the war, but later nineteenth-century archi-tecture. Looking at one of these houses, you would say that no family that entered it, with

however rosy and smiling faces, could ever come
out of it except as lean and dismal ghosts. They
look like seminaries for the production of kill-
joys. Yet, as a matter of fact, we know that
happy men, women and children have lived in
them, who played games with apples hanging
from the ceiling on Hallow-e'en, and graduated
summer after summer at the seaside from wooden
spades to iron spades and from iron spades to no
spades at all. Young men in love have walked
past house-fronts such as these and reverenced
them in fear and trembling as though angels
were watching from the windows. There may be
men so fastidious in their architectural tastes
that, having fallen in love and discovering later
that the lady dwelt in a house built of whitish-
yellow brick, would hurriedly withdraw. But,
as a rule, love laughs at architects, and, at any
rate, no unmarried woman is held responsible for
the house she lives in. She may glorify yellow
brick: yellow brick cannot dishonour her.

As for the insides of houses, anyone who has
lived much in lodgings will, as likely as not, have
lost that keen sense of personal possession of the
very walls and arrangement of a room that is felt
by many people, especially by women. I am not
indifferent to the furniture, the curtains, the
walls and the arrangement of a room, but I en-

joy these things as a spectator. I could no more arrange a room either neatly or beautifully myself than I could play the mouth-organ. I care more for the comfortableness of a chair than for its design, and I should not feel acutely miserable even if coloured Christmas supplements were hanging in frames above the mantelpiece. While I lived in a Pimlico lodging-house, I asked only two things—a lamp that would not smoke and a wicker arm-chair that would not turn a somersault when you sat down in it. My landlady had two lamps. When I complained that one of them smoked, she brought the other. When I complained that the second one smoked too, she brought back the first with a triumphant beaming "There you are, sir!" that made a fresh complaint impossible for at least forty-eight hours. Month after month, year after year, those two foul and reeking lamps marched in procession up and down the stairs, each of them always ready to take the other's place at a moment's notice. You who have never lived in lodgings may wonder that I did not indict both of the lamps at once and so get rid of them at a blow. But it is a very different thing to say to your landlady, "This lamp smokes," from saying, "All your lamps smoke." This last verges on insult and would seem like a criticism of her as a land-

lady.  If you want to live happily in lodgings, it
is essential that, on the one hand, there should
be no criticism of the landlady by you and that,
on the other, there should be no criticism of you
by the landlady.  There are generally faults on
both sides, and the less said of them the better.
Hence, though the oil-lamps smoked, and not
only smoked but were wet with spilt oil so that
they left rings and daubs of oil on the tablecloth,
on the books, on the papers—whatever they were
set down on—I endured it like a philosopher.
You could not touch one of those lamps without
becoming odorous of low-flash-point oil.  When
the lamp began to smoke as well and the smuts
to fall on your manuscripts, it was at times in-
furiating.  But youth is greatly enduring, and a
man who is not a Sybarite can live in a bed-
sitting-room with a smelling lamp well enough.

As for the chair, that was a different matter.
It was a dark brown basket-work chair, and it
leaned over a little sideways and a little backways, like a tree that has been out in many
storms.  It was probably nearing the end of its
life by the time I got to know it.  It was bowed
to such a degree that it needed only a touch for
it to topple over.  If anyone, sitting down on it,
leaned back, this shifted the centre of gravity
outside the base, and over both sitter and chair

would go, heels in air and crashing into the washstand. By sitting very carefully and remembering the insecurity of your position, you could read a book in the chair in tolerable comfort. But it did not do to get too deeply absorbed. If you ventured to forget yourself while reading *Othello*, it was on the cards that, just as the excitement reached its height, at the words "And smote him thus," you would find yourself before you could wink rolling under the washstand or into the fireplace. It was indeed a chair so tricky as to be wicked. To ask a visitor to sit down in it was like offering an unsuspecting person a mount on a savage horse. And yet, when visitors called, one always automatically offered them the most comfortable-looking chair in the room. The habit of courtesy, when once acquired, is almost impossible to get rid of. Again and again I remembered too late. I began to know most of my friends by the soles of their boots. Never can there have been a horse that flung so many human beings. In the end the thing became almost absurd. Luckily, the chair was taken away as the result of an accident. An acquaintance of mine, rather Bohemian in his ways, called on me one night to borrow money or on some equally hopeless quest. I happened to be out of London at the time and, on hearing this,

he decided to make the best of things and per-
suaded the landlord to let him borrow my room
for the night. The landlord weakly admitted
him, as he looked tired and had clearly been
drinking too much Scotch whisky. On his going
upstairs and into my room, the spectacle of a
cosy basket-work arm-chair must have been a
refreshment to exhausted eyes. The visitor seems
to have thrown himself into it whole-heartedly.
But he did not throw himself into the chair more
whole-heartedly than the chair threw him out
again. On gathering himself and the chair up
from the floor, he naturally felt that anyone who
did not know him well might be led to suspect
that he had been drinking, and, believing that
the chair was an ordinary chair that only needed
to be sat down in by a sober man, he resolved to
prove that he was sober by once more sitting
down in it. He sat down heavily, determinedly.
The chair threw him again with all the greater
violence. He set it upright again and, approaching it circumspectly, sat down with cautious
slowness. It felt all right, and he leaned back
with a smile of relief, and, as he leaned, the chair
reared and sent him flying into the washstand
again. Meanwhile my landlord sat on the stairs,
trembling with apprehension, a candle by his
side, ready to run for the fire brigade if the lamp

should be knocked over. A lady who lodged on the same floor declared the next morning that an awful fight had taken place during the night in the next room. She said it had gone on for hours, and wanted to know if anyone had been killed; she had been too terrified to cry out. As a matter of fact, there had been no fight, unless you can describe the attempt of a tipsy art student to sit down in an arm-chair as a fight. Apparently the chair won, but it was a Pyrrhic victory. The landlord and landlady, having passed a night of terror and wakefulness, agreed that, as a piece of furniture, the chair had seen its best days, and brought me in its place a spring-bottomed chair which, though perfectly safe, was a little more up-and-downish in the surface than I care for on account of its having some of the springs broken and some not. Still, the experience was a useful one in making me easily contented ever afterwards in the matter of furniture. I do not ask if a chair is Louis-Quatorze or Chippendale. I ask only whether it is possible to sit in it without pain or peril.

Still, I understand the feelings of those who, having made a house or a room beautiful, suffer at the spectacle of all this grace (which is almost a piece of their own personalities) being torn down and destroyed beyond all possibility of reconstruction. For no new house can exactly reproduce the conditions of the old. The new room may be more beautiful than the old, but the beauty of the old is gone like a flower. Sitting among the ruins the other day, and having nothing to do, I looked for something to read and found that all the books had been packed except *Paradise Lost*. It is not the most cheering book to read on the day on which one is leaving a house where one has been happy, but, for those who love houses, it is peculiarly appropriate. Not that I could read it just then. There was a deaf carpenter in the room taking down the bookshelves and breaking them up with a hammer, and to read Milton to the accompaniment of a hammer is to lose his music. It makes him too regular—too jumpily regular. I had just got to the words "Rose out of chaos" when one of the furniture-removers, going round the walls in boots that made almost more noise than hammers on the bare boards, and taking the pictures down, let one fall with a crash of broken glass on the floor. "That," said he unemotionally, "is the first to-day." I longed to be able to smile and to say, "It doesn't matter," or "It's only a little one." Theoretically, I always behave like that. But, in fact, I had a strong impulse to tell the man what I thought of him. I was restrained only by the nervousness that keeps me from telling any man what I think of him. I felt that at least he ought to have shown a little contrition. I muttered, "It can't be helped," but I muttered it in a tone that was sulky, even biting, and meant that it could easily have been helped by anybody except a clumsy fool. If it had not been so cold, I should have gone out and walked up and down beside the sprouting broccoli. But to go out would have been merely to be miserable in a different way. Seldom have I endured a day of emptier misery. After such sufferings, anyone would have been glad to get away from any house. One would have been glad even to go back to lodgings and the savageries of the arm-chair. All one asked was to be allowed to fly. . . . And now the hammers have begun in the new house. But every day new curtains go up, new fires are lit, new shelves are made secure. Soon I shall have my books in rows again, not arranged in order as in a library, but untidily as in the house of a human being. Then I shall take down *Paradise Regained* and read it (or try to), and feel perfectly content till the next flitting.

# III

## A RABBIT, A RAINBOW, AND
## A LITTLE STRIPED OWL

A RABBIT, a rainbow, and a little striped owl, all
seen within five minutes, did undoubtedly
brighten a cold and rain-soaked Easter afternoon. The world is going to the devil, as anybody may discover in the morning papers, and,
apart from that, the rain has been falling in a
deluge. Yet here comes a rabbit scampering out
of a thicket over the wet grass; here comes a rainbow, leaving its mark on a brown tumult of rain
and with its arch lost among clouds of a ghastly
whitish-grey like the skin of dead fishes; here
comes a little striped owl to its perch amid the
ruins of an ancient pear-tree, and the devil and
all his works are forgotten. One thinks less of
what the French will do next than of whether the
little owl, as he turns his head with the mechanical
precision of Punch in the show, will see that he
is being watched by a human being and will fly

away.  Alas! it is imposible not to move a little
nearer to him—to try for a closer glimpse of his
cruel eyes, of his dignified and cruel face.  He
sees better than his reputation, though it is still
daylight, and immediately dives, quiet as a
feather, and flies swiftly in the shadow of a
hedge, mounts over it as if it were a wave, and
passes swiftly down the road beyond a grove of
larches, after which there is no sign of him but
the voices of frightened birds in the distance.

He is gone, and the day is emptier for his
going.  He leaves behind him an empty world of
wet fields—fields sprinkled with young wheat
and fields that are brown and level after the
harrow—fields of all shapes and sizes lying down
the slope and climbing up the slope beyond, with
elms black in the rain and holly-trees with
scarcely more colour set irregularly on their
borders.  There is hardly a sign of spring except
in the calendar.  The earth is still mud awaiting
the word of creation.  If creation has begun, it
has not got far beyond the dog's mercury.  There
has not been such a dog's-mercury April known
for years.  The roadside is full of its green
flowers, if flowers they can be called.  They are
a sort of green porridge, and no reasonable substitute for the feast men call Spring.  Ladybirds
in their red cloaks with the seven black spots are

hiding, it is true, in the folds of their commonplace leaves.  But ladybirds cannot dominate a
landscape as dog's mercury can.  They are specks
of scarlet lost in a wilderness. . . .

That morning, as I was walking along the
edge of a ploughed field before the sun had been
drowned in the wet sky, I saw an insect that
did dominate the landscape.  It was a peacock
butterfly, with its large brown wings beating
their way along the briars and exposing eyes of
an Eastern splendour.  For a moment it seemed
as though the word of creation had been spoken
and the mud had vanished.  But immediately
afterwards the butterfly had vanished and the
mud remained.  Then something perfectly wonderful happened.  I did not believe it at first.  I
am by nature incredulous and always suspect the
first cuckoo of being a small boy.  But, a moment
later, the bird itself came into view, a cross-bow
above a wood, hurrying as ever to another hiding-
place, with its crescent-moon of wings and its
long tail.  Theoretically, I am profoundly excited
on first hearing the cuckoo.  Here is the speech
of Spring itself straight from the Equator.  In
anticipation, it is like a gift of good weather—
like the gift even of a good world.  There are
prettier songs, but none with a more magical
influence.  The cuckoo is the advance-courier of

Spring, and, at a word from him, all the soilure and darkness of winter are hurried out of sight. Everywhere is hurry and preparation for the coming of a million guests. Soon we shall have all the birds and all the butterflies and all the beetles, all the fruits and all the flowers, a pleasant congregation.

The great moments, however, have a way of being disappointing. At the voice of the first cuckoo, the windows of heaven are not really opened. Or, if they are opened, it is only to let out the rain. In the general blankness of the world, the bird seems an intruder. Its voice sounds like the voice of a cuckoo-clock—mechanical, unmysterious, conjuring up nothing outside itself. If one has a thrill of pleasure, it is not because the gaudy procession of Spring has begun to march with a cuckoo bugling at its head: it is merely because one has heard the cuckoo before anybody else of one's acquaintance. Men and women are scarcely beyond children in their pleasure at being able to say: "I saw it first," or "I heard it first." I met a man the other day who said he had seen a swallow this year. He was as modest as it is possible to be in the circumstances, but he could not entirely hide his sense of his achievement. There was no use telling him that one swallow does not make a summer. It

does at least make a summer of excitement,
especially when one talks about it afterwards.
True, it is an excitement that does not last very
long.  In a fortnight everybody will have seen
swallows, and in June if the man persists in telling people that he saw a swallow before anybody else this Spring, we shall look at him
askance as we now look at him with interest. For
the moment, he is as important as a man who
has seen something that we should all like to
have seen—the North Pole or the first days of
the Russian Revolution.  He is the focus of a
great event.  He is a go-between between us
and wonderland.  "And did you once see Shelley
plain?" cried the enthusiastic Browning.  In
our enthusiasm, we see through other men's eyes
and hear through other men's ears almost more
keenly than through our own.  Most of our en-
joyments are at second or third hand.  That is as
near as we shall ever get to the Battle of Mara-
thon or the acting of David Garrick.  Thus we
become Argus-eyed by proxy, and hear through
as many ears as Argus had eyes.  There is nothing that proves more effectively the unity of
life than the fact that in this way each of us becomes the all but universal spectator, the all but
universal auditor.  It may be that we can become
this only if we desire to see things and hear things

for ourselves. But, given the desire, we gain this power of seeing through the eyes and hearing through the ears of the human race. Nature is infinitely obliging. She cannot give us everything, but she can give us a substitute and a compensation for everything.

Even the backward Spring is not without its compensations. It contains all the more surprises. The cuckoo should not come before the chiffchaff. But this year the calendar has been turned upside down. It may be that the chiffchaffs have actually come, but have not yet begun to clip the air with their notes. Naturalists declare that they are here. It is merely that they await the rising of the curtain to sing. Spring has never learned the virtue of punctuality—if indeed it is a virtue, seeing that it is not in nature. There is, no doubt, a sort of regularity in nature which may seem to excuse the deification of punctuality, but it is a regularity that allows of an infinite variety. The sun does not rise at the same hour on three successive days. Spring seldom begins on the day officially given in Letts's diaries. It is an example of our gross human impudence that we should attempt to bind it down to a fixed time like a music-hall performance. Nature is neither a music-hall performer nor a business man, but a

poet. It works by inspiration, not by the clock.
The year is a circle, but it is never the same circle.
That, perhaps, is why it is one of 'he few circles
that are eternally interesting. Its variety makes
us interested in seeing things not happening as
well as in seeing things happening—in seeing
spring weather that intimidates even chaffinches
into silence, save for their tinny winter hiccup.
Amid the drearness of dell and thornbush, the
song of the wren hidden in the wet branches
seems all the more triumphant. It is a song
brilliant as a rainbow in a wet sky—brilliant as
a dance of rainbows. There is a shameless optimism in it that clothes the bare hedges with
something better than leaves. There is no other
resident bird so incapable of melancholy. The
robin is often pensive, and sings to us and looks
down at us from the apple-tree as though he
sympathised with us. But the wren never sings
except to say that it is the best of all possible
worlds. His must have been the voice that first
sounded immediately after God saw that it was
all very good. The wren is the incarnate Amen
of creation. He has moods of anger, it is true,
when his grating voice can be heard in the hedge,
and he has moments of mild fear, when his little
brown form scurries ahead of one, five yards at a
time, among the thorns of the lane. But, when

the danger is past, he recovers his spirits and
raises his song with an exaggerated boastfulness.
"The wren, the wren, the king of all birds," an
old country rhyme begins. He certainly swells
into a king in his song. If Noah had put his
cock wren out on the roof of the Ark, the flood
would no longer have seemed a barren waste, but
would have scintillated for him as the thing his
imagination had desired.

Every charming thing, indeed, gains in a
measure from a background of barrenness. The
stitchwort opening out of its green sheath into a
white star on the roadside attracts us all the more
because it is in a solitude of weeds. Child calls
to child and points to the half-hidden purple
glow of the ground ivy all the more eagerly because of its rarity. And how delightful to come
on the periwinkle creeping over a bank in a blue
cloud! The earth is still winter's, but these are
spring's. Spring's, too, is the gentle oscillating
voice of the hedge-sparrow, and the red flowers
mixed with the cones of the larch. Even the be-
lated marsh-tit, with its exquisite mushroom-
brown wings, that rocks and taps in the coco-nut,
is an embodied anticipation of spring. As for the
blue-tit, seen from below, he is a Chinese curiosity with his parti-coloured face. But when he
alights on the ground beside the bacon-rind that

has been thrown out for him and we see his back, we begin to wonder whether there was ever such a painted thing in nature. We do not know how beautiful birds are till we have seen them from above. If one has never seen a swallow's blue back, one cannot be said ever to have seen a swallow. The blue-tit is not so rich in colour— the deep colour of summer seas. He is prettiness compared to beauty, but of what a dazzling prettiness!

And so the day passed—an interval of reading, an interval of eating, an interval of conversation, and an interval of walking, with a peewit flying so close above my head that I heard the creak of its wings, and two wild ducks hurrying with their long necks high above the trees in the lonely sky. Nor did I enjoy the walk the less because I was within half-a-mile of the "Cupid" —the "Cupid" that is so remote from the speech of town that, if you ask for beer, the landlady inquires: "Ale or stout?" The bottle of beer she brought me was the last in the small house, so that I had perforce to try the stout—black as the wet trees and more comforting. Then I went home, and saw the rabbit, the rainbow and the little striped owl. Then I went in and read Schopenhauer. "Life," I read, "oscillates between pain and boredom." And again: "All na-

tions speak ill of each other, and all are right."
There is something to be said for Schopenhauer.
There is something to be said for the song of the
wren.  And it may be that there is something to
be said for bottled stout.

## IV

## KEEPING THE SABBATH

NOTHING could be more paradoxical than the English attitude to Sunday. England has now for a generation or so kept the Sabbath in public and broken it in private. As a consequence, strict Sabbatarians, though they have deplored a certain laxity in the English observance of the Sabbath, have been able to delude themselves into believing that in this matter Protestant England was at least not nearly so bad as Catholic Ireland. Orange writers, indeed, in comparing Ireland with England, have constantly attributed the woes of the Irish to the fact that they are a nation of Sabbath-breakers. As a matter of fact, Ireland is almost as much addicted to Sabbath observance as Scotland— infinitely more so than England—but in a different way. In Ireland, everybody goes to church once on Sunday; in Scotland, everybody goes twice, or ought to; in England, hardly anybody goes at all. The Irishman may attend a political meeting or a hurling match on Sunday afternoon, but his conscience would prick him if in the morning he had not been to say his "mouthful of prayers" in the chapel. Thus the Irish may be described as a nation of church-going Sabbath-breakers, while the English break the Sabbath without troubling to go to church. As I have said, however, they have hitherto broken it in private without breaking it too badly in public. The theatres, the cricket grounds and the football fields have slept in a Sabbath peace, even if young men and maidens have crept unobtrusively to the tennis lawns or gone for picnics on the river where there are no clergymen, or bathed or fished from the piers on the Sussex coast. Citizens have done this, as it were, at their own risk. Sabbath-breaking has not yet been organised as on the Continent, but merely connived at. And yet the thin end of the wedge has during the past thirty or forty years been ever advancing from thickness to thickness. Sunday concerts and Sunday excursions have been becoming more and more numerous. Sunday bands in the parks were succeeded by the Sunday opening of museums and art galleries, and this in turn was followed by Sunday cinemas. It is scarcely a generation since public opinion was so profoundly shocked by the decision of *The Daily Telegraph* and *The Daily Mail* to publish Sunday newpapers that the attempt was hurriedly abandoned. Yet to-day even the clergyman reads his Sunday paper before going off to conduct the morning service. He probably learned to do so during the war. After all, if it was right to blow human beings to pieces with high-explosive shells on Sunday, the Recording Angel was hardly going to waste ink in writing reports about people who merely sat at home and read about it in a Sunday newspaper. It is probable, however, that even without the war public opinion in favour of Sunday observance was ceasing to have any effective existence. Society was indifferent to the Sabbath; the working classes were indifferent to it; the younger generation was indifferent. As the habit of church-going declined, more and more people were bound to demand some form of activity to take its place. Even the clergy have begun to see in large numbers that the alternative ways of spending Sunday are no longer church-going minus recreation and recreation minus church-going, but are church-going plus recreation and recreation minus church-going. They have ceased to expect to save the Sabbath as a whole, in the old sense. The most they can hope for is to save a piece of it, as in Catholic countries. In another fifty years, I fancy, most of the Christian Churches will have accepted the theory that the Sabbath is a Jewish rather than a Christian institution, and Sabbatarianism will be as rare as the objection to instrumental music in the house of God.

The decision of the London County Council to allow cricket and football and other games in the public places under its control on Sunday merely translates public opinion into action. And if there is to be a religious revival in the future, it must be a revival that will save the souls of people who play games on Sunday as well as people who work in factories and offices on weekdays. Even so, many of us will be unable to bid the old-fashioned Sabbath farewell without a mild sentiment of regret. We did not wish it to stay, but we cannot see it go without a note almost of tenderness in our leave-taking. It was not, now that we can think of it without bitterness, entirely a tyrant and a kill-joy. How hideous it was in town with those tinny church bells making a noise as musical as an orchestra of buckets, dinning into us that we must hurry and put our boots on and leave our breakfast half finished, or we should be late for the church from which we would gladly have stayed away!

The very pavements seemed dull under our hast-
ing feet.  Every shop we passed had its shutters
up as if its eyes were closed in a pretence of
prayer.  Houses frowned. solemn as humbugs.
The streets were empty of the pleasant hum of
people going hither and thither on their natural
activites.  Men in unnatural silk hats, boys in
unnatural bowlers, everybody wearing gloves or
carrying them, everybody dressed as if wishing
to prove that it was possible to be a Christian and
yet to look like a lady or gentleman, many with
Bibles, Prayer Books, and bags with scent
bottles—was there ever so dreary a procession to
join for a boy who would rather have been lying
in bed or going for a walk into the country?  It
is true that the people were a great deal more
cheerful coming from church than going to it.
After the Benediction they became almost merry.
They did not do more than twinkle at each
other as they shook hands and whispered their
"How are you's" within the sacred building.
But, as they passed out of the porch and down
the wide steps, their whispers rose into speech,
they made jokes and laughed, and they went out
of the gates and along the street in the jollity
of universal benevolence.  No one who has ever
gone to church will easily forget the thrill of
coming out of it—the hat hastily seized, the fresh

air already breathed in anticipation as one joined
the slow procession down the aisle, the men holding their hats high, everybody walking at half-
a-mile an hour on his legs and yet hurrying,
hurrying, into the outside world in his spirit.

But it would be false to suggest that one never
enjoyed being in church except when one was
leaving it. It was the theory of going to church
rather than the practice of it that came like a
darkness over the morning. To hear the Scriptures beautifully read—"Arise, my love, my fair
one, and come away," or "O my son Absalom,
my son, my son Absalom, would God I had died
for thee. Absalom, my son, my son," or "Consider the lilies of the field"—was to be thrilled
as one has never been thrilled since, except by
great actors speaking great words on the stage.
And there were sermons, too, that were works
of art—sermons that seemed to be spoken, as
Isaak Walton said of Donne's by an angel out
of a cloud. The best of them, perhaps, were
sermons about death—sermons that touched us
with the universal sorrow and made each of us
feel a sojourner and stranger among the games
and the landscapes of earth. How insecure we
felt—like a tiny group, helplessly huddled on a
raft, and with the threat of storms and savage
seas that would engulf us! But the very hope-

lessness of our plight made the reassuring words
at the end come with a sweetness that stilled the
air into an extraordinary silence: "Fear not, little
flock. Lo, I am with you always, even unto the
end of the world. . . ." It may be that one
looked on as at a spectacle—that one sympathised with the little flock, not as one of them, but
as with characters on the stage. Still, one envied
them, if not in their lives, in their salvation.
One stood apart, like the young man with great
possessions, hesitating between two worlds,
stirred by the beauty of the one and bound fast
by the beauty of the other. There is something
to be said for the view that, as church-going de-
clines, children will be the poorer both in experience and education. They may be released from
a tyranny, but they will also be deprived of an
early initiation into the arts and much that the
arts stand for. Church-going has narrowed
many a mind but it has also brought many
a mind into touch with the great tradition
that took over the civilisation of Europe from
the Greeks and the Romans. Besides this, even
the leaping tongues of Hell-fire gave some kind
of a cosmic background to the imagination. And
for most of us these were not nearly so terrifying
as is sometimes made out. We had a Micaw-
berish hope that something would turn up to save

us from the worst on the Last Day.  After all,
one could repent in middle age, when life would
have so few pleasures that one would lose very
little by becoming a Christian.

But Sunday was a complete day of delight
only in the country, and only in some places in
the country.  There was a peace in the morning
air that seemed to affect even the birds in the
trees—even the leaves on the trees.  The bees
flew about the hedges in a still air that intensified
each individual humming so that it passed, like a
melody suddenly swept out of the silence and on
into the silence again.  The happiest days were
those on which there was not enough room in the
trap for everybody to go to church, and somebody had to stay at home and it was one's own
turn to do so.  How pleasant it was to help to
yoke the horse, to hold up the shafts, to fix the
trace, to find the right hole for the britchen-strap!
How pleasant to stand in the yard and see the
packed churchgoers turn out of the gate, smiling
farewells!  One would almost have liked to be
with them; but the theory of staying away from
church was too overwhelmingly attractive.  Then
there was the walk with a cousin through
the fields, each of them with its memorable name
—the Causeway Field, the Whin Field, the
Swine's Knowe, Lime-kiln Land.  There is no

idleness to compare with such a Sunday-morning saunter. There is not a sign of man's energy or labour in all the miles of prospect. To-day the very horses rest from their labours and shake their incompetent tails as they munch the grass in the fields. To-day the lamb is safe from the butcher's eye, and the crops grow in a world of idle and harmless men. If one meets a man walking along beside the hedge, he is a country-man chewing a grass and ambling more slowly than a cow, letting his large feet fall lazily on the ground rather than using them for any pur-pose of progression. There are mutual jests about not being at church, a secret twinkle of self-congratulation in the eyes of each, a refer-ence to an old dying man—"He was very bad last night"—and a new version of what Sarah had said to Johnnie when he came home without the wages. If politics were talked, it would be about Gladstone and Home Rule and Roman Catholics, who were superstitious people who broke the Sabbath. But the man chewing the grass might himself be a Catholic, and then there would be no politics talked, but only friendly gossip about people and cattle and cricket and what happened at the wake the night before last. It was a perfectly animal existence, but how per-fectly satisfying! And in the afternoon one

would walk down to the sandy river-mouth and
play shoulder-stone with the foreign gipsies,
whose very children just out of the cradle smoked
pipes and cigarettes. It was not, perhaps, without a sense of sin that one allowed the gipsies to
perform their star turn of muzzling a bear they
had with them and setting a dog to fight it. This
was breaking the Sabbath in good earnest, and
the memory of the story of Elisha and of the
capacity of bears for destroying wicked children
was not reassuring. The gipsies roared with delight every time the monster roared, but there
was one boy who looked on a little anxiously.
Then there was the walk home in time for the
evening prayers, everybody reading a verse in
sequence, if it were only, "And Abraham begat
Isaac," and an illiterate servant spelling the
words out in a loud sing-song. . . . Yes, one
feels tenderly towards the Sabbath, now that it
is gone. One would not like to have missed it.
One feels rather sorry for the coming generation
that it will know nothing of the joys either of
keeping or of breaking the holy day.

## V

## CONVERSATION

I⊤ is said that the art of conversation is dead, but
if you are staying at a hotel and go into the bar
after returning from the pictures you will find
that there are still places where men carry on
quite wonderful conversations till midnight. I
spent a night at a town not far from Cowes during Regatta week, and I heard a conversation
that left no doubt in my mind that Swift and
Pope and Gay have their successors in modern
England. I do not know how the talk drifted
from Bottomley, whom a little lean-faced com-
mercial traveller drinking bitter in the corner
refused to "'it when 'e's down," to King George,
but for about ten minutes a chorus of male voices
discussed the King and the hard life he leads—
Goodwood one week, Cowes the next, and never
a day idle. "I was watching him at Goodwood,"
said a young Jew in blue trousers and fawn-
coloured socks, "and saw him shakeen hands,

shakeen hands, with about thirty people in five minutes, toucheen his hat and boween—greeteens, I suppose you would call it. I thought to myself I'd rather be dead. Greeteens, greeteens all the time." "W'y does 'e do it?" the lean little man asked; "it's all 'umbug." "Of course it's humbug," replied the Jew warmly; "and nobody knows it better than the King. That's what makes it such hard work." "That's what I mean," interrupted the landlord, a large, fat man with a moustache, a bowler on the back of his head, and a booming voice, "when I call him a harassed man. I don't suppose there's a man what's more harassed in the whole of England than King George. I wouldn't take his job, not if you paid me for it." "Give me the Prince of Wales," a spectacled Scotsman in a mackintosh mumbled into his moustache, without taking his pipe out of his mouth. "Ah, the Prince," said the landlord, wagging his head; "he's hot—hot as mustard. A naval officer what was with him in India was telling me the other night how he routed that fellow Gandhi." "Who's he?" asked the Jew. "Gandhi?" said the landlord: "you know, the agitator. Well, as I was saying, the Prince of Wales, as soon as he got to India, said, 'Look here, I'm going to interview that fellow.' Of course, everybody was scared blue. 'You can't,' they told him. 'You'll only be shot if you try.' 'I don't give a damn,' says the Prince of Wales; 'go and fix up an appointment.' And they had to. Well, the result was the appointment was made, and the Prince drove off as bold as a lion to keep it. Well, when he got there, there was no Gandhi." "What happened?" mumbled the Scotsman. "What happened?" repeated the landlord in a voice of exasperation. "He'd bunked, run away, took to his heels. I reckon there isn't another man living who could have done what the Prince of Wales done. By gosh! he's hot—hot as mustard."

A genial little man in a brown bowler hat who had not been saying much looked up from the sofa on which he was sitting at the clock. "Coming on to midnight, gentlemen," he said; "I hope everybody here will remember to say 'Rabbit, rabbit, rabbit, first thing in the morning. Rabbit, rabbit, rabbit," he repeated the words as if to impress them on our memory. "Rabbit, rabbit, rabbit," the lean traveller tried the words over as if testing them to see if they had any meaning; "I don't get the 'ang of it." "Why," the man in the brown hat laughed at him, "I thought everybody knew 'Rabbit, rabbit, rabbit.' If you say 'Rabbit, rabbit, rabbit'—three times, just like that—first thing in the morning on the first of

the month, even before you say your prayers,
you'll get a present before the end of the month."
"Supposin' you don't say any prayers," the lean
traveller objected. "Well, it's all the same," the
other assured him; "say 'Rabbit, rabbit, rabbit'
before you say anything else, and I guarantee
you'll get a present before the end of the month."
"Rabbit, rabbit, rabbit," said the Jew in the
fawn-coloured socks. "Well, I'm damned!"
"Supposin' we sit 'ere till twelve o'clock, does
that count?" asked the lean traveller. "Yes,"
replied the brown hat, "that counts. Say 'Rabbit, rabbit, rabbit'—three times—first thing after
twelve o'clock, and you'll get a present as sure
as I'm drinking this glass of bitter." "Rabbit,
rabbit, rabbit," the Scotsman repeated the words
in a sepulchral voice; "I never heard that before." "Well," the spokesman for the superstition told him, "try it. To-morrow's the first of
August. When you're called in the morning, you
mustn't even answer till you've said 'Rabbit, rabbit, rabbit.' If you remember to do that,
you'll find that what I'm telling you is true."
"Rabbit, rabbit, rabbit," the Scotsman once
more repeated solemnly, and, having done so,
raised his glass of whisky solemnly to his
lips. "Supposin' you said 'Chicken, chicken,
chicken?'" inquired the lean man. "It's no

good," the other assured him: "there's nothing
any good, only 'Rabbit, rabbit, rabbit.'" "Did
you ever try this yourself?" a black-moustached
man with drink-weary eyes inquired. "Often,"
said the other, "and always got a present."
"Always got a present," the Scotsman echoed
him, and took another drink of whisky. "What
d'you mean by a present?" the lean man
asked. "If a man stood you a whisky-and-
soda, would that be a present?" "No," said the
other after a moment's reflection, "I think the
present has to be a real present. It might be a
hundred pounds, or it might be a box of choco-
lates. Don't forget it. 'Rabbit, rabbit, rabbit.'
Never been known to fail." "There are some curious superstitions," said the man with the black
moustache. "Are you one of the people who
object to seeing the new moon through glass?"
"God!" said the other, "I wouldn't like to see
the new moon through glass." "*I* believe," said
the Jew, "that it's unlucky to fall downstairs on
a Friday—or any other day"; and he sniggered
at his wit. "Rabbit, rabbit, rabbit," said the man
in the brown hat, yawning; "that's the best of
them. You can't go wrong with it." "Rabbit,
rabbit, rabbit," the Scotsman meditated, blinking
his eyes, and the faint shadow of a smile stealing
into his features. "You've got it," the other

nodded approval; "rabbit, rabbit, rabbit." "Rabbit, rabbit, rabbit," the Scotsman smiled outright; "and you get a present? That's very good."

I cannot remember how the talk found its way to the subject of village life; but I remember the Jew telling a long story of how, when he was passing the night in a Sussex village, he made the villagers so drunk that, after closing time, they gathered outside the hotel and sang a bawdy version of *In Sussex by the Sea*. He sang the chorus over in a sort of whisper for our delectation, laughed heartily, and said that it struck him as being "damned funny." "Funny things you see in some villages," said the landlord, with a dreamy look. "A friend of mine—he's dead now, poor chap—got a stoppage of the bowels— bought a little pub in a village like the one you mention. It lay just off the main road, but those few yards made all the difference. All the motor cars and traffic passed the end of the road without knowing the pub even existed, and my friend was doing no business, absolutely. 'Look here, Bill,' I said to him, 'I'll tell you what to do. Go down to the cross-roads, and, whenever you see a motor car, put up your hand, and, when it stops, say, "Come along, gents, to the Pink Horse, and have a drink for nothing." They'll think you're balmy, of course, but some o' 'em will come, and anyhow people will get to know about you.' Poor Bill stood at the cross-roads for hours, but he could get only one man to come along to the pub, and *he* wasn't looking half scared." The landlord laughed at the memory. "Then," he went on, "I thought I'd better go out myself and see if I couldn't get a move on. Well, I made up my mind to offer a drink to every Tom, Dick and Harry I could see. If I saw a motor car I stopped it and said: 'Come along, gents; be sports. I'm having a little house-warming, and I want you to be my guests for the day.' The funniest thing was an old tramp who was carrying his dinner in a handker-chief. When I told him to go up to the Pink Horse and he could have as much drink as he wanted for nothing, he looked as if he wanted to escape. 'I'm not balmy,' I told him; 'it's true. Here'—and I pulled out a two-shilling piece from my pocket—'take that, if you don't believe me, and go and spend it in the Pink Horse if you can.' Oh! it was a rare day. We even got the village policeman in. He was a teetotaller, the beast. But he said he didn't mind a bottle of stone ginger. Well, I was drinking ginger beer myself, with a drop of gin in it. So what did I do but slip a drop of gin into his too. Well, it was a hot day, and he had another one, and another one, and another one. He liked it, the brute, like a cat likes milk. Oh! he was proper oiled before the night was through. I tell you, by the time we had to put the lights out we had that village painted as tight as a drum. Absolutely. Tight? They were singing *God save the King* backways." "I like about the policeman," said the Jew with the socks; "swine most of them are." "Well," said the landlord broad-mindedly, "there's policemen are swine, and there's policemen isn't. I once had a place in a little Australian village where the policeman was a brick. Do you know, he was there for twenty-five years, and there were only two convictions? And I was responsible for one of them. I saw a man slashing a horse about with a stick, tearing the poor beast in a most horrible manner, and I took him by the throat and ran him into the station myself. The old policeman didn't want me to charge him. He said there'd only be trouble. But I said, 'He's a cruel brute. I want to see him taught a lesson.' Well, next day he was had up, and the magistrate fined him five dollars. And do you know what happened? The old policeman I'm telling you about paid the fine out of his own pocket. 'You oughtn't to do it,' I told him; 'the man's a dirty devil.' 'I know he is,' said the policeman; 'it's not out of any sympathy with him I paid the fine. It was the principle of the thing. You see, there has only been one conviction in the village for twenty-five years, and that was a poor devil I felt sorry for, so I paid his fine to keep him from being sent to prison. And, now that I'm just going to retire, here comes the second conviction, and, thinking of the old time, I says to myself, "It's not worth breaking a rule just when you're going to retire. You paid the only other fine: you should pay this one." You see what I mean, sir; it's the principle of the thing.' I thought that funny, him feeling, just because he had once done a thing, he had to go on doing it." "Rabbit, rabbit, rabbit," the Scotsman was chuckling to himself, practising for the morning. The landlord took no notice of him. "Well, when he retired," he went on, "the new policeman was a holy terror. He was another brute of a teetotaller, and it came to this, you could hardly light your pipe without being arrested. He used to stand in the shadow under a balcony at night to watch what people were doing. One night, just before going to bed, I was leaning out of the window, and saw where he was standing in the darkness. I couldn't resist it. I got an egg and flung it hard as I could—click!—right at his eye, and smashed it all over his face.  A minute later he was knocking rat-a-tat-tat at the door, and I went down to see what he wanted. 'Well?' I said to him. 'Somebody threw an egg at me,' he said, 'and I think it was from your house.' 'How dare you?' said I; 'do you accuse me of doing it?  How dare you come knocking me up and me dressed for bed, merely because you happen to have a mean, suspicious mind!  I only wish it *had* been me threw the egg.  And hit you.  Nothing would have pleased me better.' And I slammed the door in his face.  Of course, he could do nothing.  He had no evidence.  Soon after that he had to leave the village.  Things were made too hot for him, and he got his face cut about most horrible by a man wearing a stirrup like a knuckle-duster.  Oh! he was a proper drop of poison!" . . .

It was now getting near midnight, and the Scotsman was obviously getting anxious to retire into the seclusion of his own room in order to qualify for his present when the clock struck. Everybody made a move bedwards. "Don't forget," the man in the brown hat gave us the parting injunction. " 'Rabbit, rabbit, rabbit,' three times. Good-night, gentlemen." "Good-night." "Good-night." "Good-night." "Good-night."

# VI

## ODD VOLUMES

IT is a curious habit, the habit of collecting books. It is not by any means the same thing as the habit of reading. Most of us who have bookshelves collect scores—perhaps hundreds—of volumes that we shall never read. We keep them as a kind of store of knowledge. They are to us what money at the bank is to a financier. They are a second brain, and we feel that, if our own brain fails, we can call in the aid of these reserves on our shelves. To possess the *Encyclopædia Britannica* alone gives many men this confidence. Even the *Encyclopædia Britannica,* however, cannot allay the appetite of a man who has once become generally acquisitive of books. If anything, it sharpens his appetite. It teaches him of the existence of subjects of which he had probably never before heard, leading him from stereo-isomerism to palæobotany. I am, I suspect, a person with unusually small powers of resist-

ance and am more easily tempted by a subject
of which I shall never know anything than most
men would be in the same circumstances. How
else can I explain the presence on my shelves of
such books as *The Naga Tribes of Manipur, The
Mafulu Mountain People of New Guinea,* and
*Man and Beast in Eastern Ethiopia?* It may be
thought that I suffer from a suppressed wish to
travel in wild places and, perhaps, to hunt tigers
and rhinoceroses. I should be more inclined to
consider this explanation if it were not that I can
see, not far from these volumes, other volumes of
such an entirely different character as *The A B
C of Collecting Old English Pottery, Heraldry
for Amateurs,* and *The Child Welfare Movement.* Then there are books about Greek sculp-
ture, about ancient Egyptian religion, about
socialism, about birds, about gardening, about
the French Revolution, about Shakespeare,
about auction bridge, about poetry, about as-
tronomy, about Ireland, about butterflies, about
ideals, about Japanese prints, about the Bible,
about books, about numismatics, about Bergson.
There is no more reason in the collection than in
the alphabet. I cannot explain how I came to
make such a collection, unless it is that somewhere there is hidden in me a Faust with the
desire for universal knowledge. It is as though I

had said to myself: "Some day—though not just now—I shall take down and read *Astrology and Religion among the Greeks and Romans.*" And so on, through a thousand volumes. To have a shelf of such books is to enjoy a great deal of potential reading. It is for the pleasures of potential reading that I keep a copy of *The Confessions of St. Augustine* in the original Latin. It is still uncut save for the first eight pages, and I have no doubt I shall put off cutting the rest of it till some fine, idle, sunny afternoon in eternity. To possess a book of this kind is its own reward. Perhaps the book means even more to me on account of my not having read it. At present it is not an achievement, but a hope, a perpetual promise. After all, to have read a book is to have vulgarised it. It is to have exchanged Samarcand for Southend—the unknown for the known.

It is a strange fact that unread books go on accumulating for years, unchallenged and almost unnoticed, until one moves into another house. At such a crisis, one is amazed to find what very queer fish have contrived to squeeze themselves into places on the shelves. I was not surprised last week to see on my shelves a large book of nearly six hundred pages called *Hermeneutic Interpretation of the Origin of the Social State*

*of Man and of the Destiny of the Adamic Race.*
Anyone might take home a book like that to find
out what the title meant. Besides, who, if he
opened the book, could resist such a chapter
heading as "Orpheus, Moses, and Fo-hi; Who
They Were." Who could resist, I mean, putting
it on his shelves? It is perfectly easy to resist
reading it. But the books that it has surprised
me most to find on my shelves are the books on
health and medicine. I am all the more surprised
because I never read books on medicine. I do
not mind confessing to an occasional dip into a
reference book which gives all the diseases in
alphabetical order with a description of their
symptoms. I have been spared many an anxious
night through taking it down and discovering
that an occipital headache does not necessarily
mean what I thought it meant. The sort of medical books, however, of which I find to my astonishment that my shelves are full are books with
names like *What Shall I Eat?* and *How to Live
Long.* I got rid of *Self-Help for Nervous Women* some years ago. I gave it and *With a Dog-
Sleigh in Canada* to a woman's suffrage bazaar.
The lady who ran the stall told me afterwards
that she sold both books to the same person, who
said, as she took up *With a Dog-Sleigh in
Canada:* "This will do for the spare bedroom."

Possibly it was for the haunted room that she bought *Self-Help for Nervous Women.* Now I had been keeping that book for years; I do not know why. I do not know any nervous women— at least I never met a woman who was half so nervous as I am myself. As for *What Shall I Eat?* it can be said in its favour that the subject is a good one. Probably, when I took it home, I thought it was full of descriptions of the sort of delicacies that you see in Fortnum & Mason's windows. Alas, on looking through the book lately when owing to a flitting I had to make a clearance of some hundreds of volumes, I found that it might as well have been called *What Shall I Not Eat?* Pages are wasted on such subjects as bread and potatoes. Thus, when the appetite craves for something like a Ritz dinner, the author solemnly harps on such things as this:

"Bread is for all, hale or ailing, the fundamental element of alimentation. From the physiological standpoint the man who performs manual labour requires a large quantity of it. So far as pathological conditions are concerned, we know of no disease in which the use of bread is especially indicated; but there are such in which, by retaliation, as it were, it is badly tolerated and may even prove harmful."

No doubt it is a good book for those who wish

to read that sort of thing. I confess I prefer Plutarch or Wordsworth or Edgar Wallace. I do
not wish to be told that "the action of eggs on
the liver has given rise to endless discussion," or
that:

"If large quantities are eaten, eggs may become injurious, as the liver becomes surcharged
not only with nitrogenous bodies, but also with
fat and lecithin. Chemical analysis of *foies gras*
shows how quickly lecithin is accumulated in the
liver."

It makes me melancholy to think that I have
for years been giving house-room to this sort of
stuff under a misapprehenion. The last man in
the world whose opinion I would take on what
to eat would be a doctor. It is far safer to consult
a waiter, and not a bit more expensive.

There are other books of a medical kind, however, which I have been delighted to discover
lately on my shelves. I have thrown away many
books in the last fortnight, but I have not thrown
away *A Stitch in Time*. Just as I was about to
throw it away, I opened it by chance at the cure
for hiccup, which runs:

"Draw in deep breaths, holding them as long
as possible. If this fails, pull tongue out with
handkerchief and place a piece of salt or soda
bicarbonate on the back of it. Continue to hold

the tongue out for a few minutes. Put mustard plaster on stomach."

I am not sure that, in certain cases, treatment so drastic would not be resented. It is not everyone—even in the genial afterglow of a City banquet—who would allow you to pull out his tongue with a handkerchief and to place a piece of salt or soda bicarbonate on the back of it. It is not even everyone who would allow you without protest to put a mustard plaster on his stomach. Thus, this volume of "Simple and Practical Remedies and Suggestions for Use when a Physician cannot be Immediately Secured and in Cases Considered too Trivial for Professional Care" may well fail at the first impact of its advice on real life.

The first chapter of this admirable book is called "Miscellaneous Casualties," and it covers a number of the more terrifying things that may happen to us, from dog and snake bites to "nose bleed." One of the most useful paragraphs is headed "Swallowing Buttons, Coins, etc." It begins:

"If lodged in throat remove with forceps, piece of wire, crochet needle, or by a sharp slap on the back with patient's head and arms hanging down. Infants can easily be inverted, holding by legs."

What seems odd to an ordinary reader is that

writers of books of this kind take it for granted
that a piece of wire can be got hold of in less
time than a doctor. I confess, if at a crisis I
were suddenly told to go and fetch a piece of
wire, I should not know how to set about it. I
could, no doubt, if given time enough, discover
a hardware merchant's, but even then I should
not care to order less than a yard, as a smaller
quantity would look mean, and a yard of wire
would be far too long to put down a child's throat
unless it had actually swallowed the button. On
the whole, I prefer the alternative mode of
treatment, for, as the author of *A Stitch in Time*
reminds us, "infants can easily be inverted,
holding by legs."

Dipping into the book, I came on a number of
other curious pieces of information in the chapter
called "Everyday Troubles," among which, I regret to find, are included cracked toes, lumbago
and boils, but the following chapter of "General
Information and Hints" pleased me still more on
account of the kindly spirit in which the reader
is told how to take care of a hot-water bottle.
There is too much thoughtlessness in the common
attitude to hot-water bottles. The author of
*A Stitch in Time* would have us treat them as
considerately as a little girl treats her doll.
Thus:

*"Fill bottle* only a third full. Lay bottle length-wise on flat surface, holding neck up, allowing water to fill neck. Expel all air by gently patting the bottle. Screw on cork and invert. Dry off and make sure of no leakage. Put cover on or wrap in towel."

Could anything be more sympathethic, more humane? And, indeed, there is nothing responds more quickly to humane treatment than a hot-water bottle. Treat it roughly, flood it with boiling water, and it will struggle, kick, and give great gasping sobs, and, as likely as not, burn the hand that feeds it. Treat it tenderly, and pat it gently while filling it with water of exactly the right heat, and it will purr like a kitten. I once knew a man who called his hot-water bottle "Willie," and who used to talk to it, as he filled it, as if it had been a pet animal.

The worst of it is, however, if one begins to read the books one finds on one's shelves, one has no time to get rid of them. And, delightful as it is to hurl books on a heap to be thrown away, how much more delightful it is to open one of them casually and to come on such a passage as I have just come on in *Man's Best Food:*

"Chrysippos, a Stoic (282-209 B.C.), considered that animals had reasoning powers. Democritus, and after him Pliny, ascribed moral

characteristics and religious feeling to ele-
phants."

The discovery of such a passage confirms one
in the belief that there is probably a sentence in
every book that makes it worth preserving. I
have to exert my will to keep from peeping
between the covers of some of these monsters in
two volumes for fear I should find something
interesting in them, and not have the heart to
add them to the sacrificial pile. You may think
it impossible to find anything interesting in a
book in two volumes, but I remember doing so
several times.

# VII

## LONDONERS

It is the mark of a townsman to feed birds. No one in the country would think of feeding birds, except caged birds, or tits, or pigeons, or fowls, or during a frost. There is food, indeed, in every tree and in every garden and in every field. To throw breadcrumbs to birds in such circumstances would be merely a rather ridiculous hobby, like flinging pennies to be scrambled for by peers on their way to the House of Lords. In London conditions are changed. Here the birds are beggars and dependent on our charity. The black-headed gulls swoop down in procession by Blackfriars Bridge, each with a beggar's whine. The ducks in the parks stand on their heads for halfpence. The sparrows, if you have so much as a crust of bread on you, will gather round you like guttersnipes demanding "mouldies." Many people speak ill of sparrows. I can understand dislike of them in the country, but I cannot understand it in the town. In the country they are invaders, driving out of the neighbourhood

62

better birds than themselves. Other birds apparently regard them as low, and will not consort in the same garden with them. They will not, at least, make friends, and they have a happier air when the sparrows are gone. In town, on the other hand, the sparrow is at home. He does not keep the other birds away, for they would not come in any case. He has no music for the traffic to drown—no bright plumage for the smoke to blacken. He is a little parasite, who can pick up a living where a more sensitive bird would starve. He is cheeky, Cockney, insuppressible. He is, in a sense, vicious. He will go through a bed of crocuses and break their necks with as little compunction as a fox destroying geese. It would not be so bad if he really wanted to eat the crocuses, but it is as though he actually enjoyed wasting them. He leaves them lying, yellow, and purple and white, like a battle-field of flowers. No cat was ever more cruel. But, apart from this, I do not see what can be said against him by the townsman. How charming a little dancer he is as he hops in scores and in fifties round a Londoner who has bread—hops backwards and forwards like a marionette or like someone whose feet have been tied together for fun, or like a small child hoping up and down in sheer excitement. He may not, as an individual, be so confiding as the robin.  But the robins do not come dancing round a human being in families like the family of the old woman who lived in a shoe.  They are selfish birds, and no robin will share a human being with another robin.  Sparrows are sociable, like a crowd of children begging from a tourist.  They may be greedy; they may fight over the spoils; but their vices are the vices of creatures that love the company of their kind.

The seagull, however, seems to me to be a more interesting London bird than the sparrow.  The seagull is a bird that can spy a piece of bread almost as far as a vulture can spy a corpse.  It is impossible to enter one of the London parks with a piece of dry bread in your pocket without every seagull knowing it for a mile around.  I was standing by the Round Pond the other day, when a small girl came up with a paper bag full of bread to feed the ducks.  She opened the bag and, taking out a slice that had seen better days, said to me gravely, "Would *you* like a bit?"  I felt it would be ungracious to refuse, and no sooner had she passed me the slice of bread than a cloud of gulls came falling down out of the sky, each gull with a different-sized brown patch on its head.  They whirled about us with such clamour that there was nothing to be done but

begin to feed them. I have never before thrown
bread at seagulls, but I found it extraordinarily
satisfying. It was like watching the most brilliant possible fielding at cricket.[1]

It may be that in time one learns to distinguish
between the cleverness of one bird and the cleverness of another in catching fragments of bread
on the wing. Sometimes a catch is missed, and
the bread has to be retrieved from among the
ducks in the water. But as a rule one of the birds
proves its genius by breaking out of the crowd
and intercepting the bread at the beginning of
its fall with open beak. There is certainly
enough variety of catching and missing to pre-
vent feeding the seagulls from ever becoming
tedious. It would, I fancy, be rather monotonous
if it were not for this constant element of doubt.
Every time one throws bread into the air, however, one has a sort of gambler's interest in what
is going to happen. One is playing with the
unknown. The permutations and combinations
of chance are as numerous, perhaps, in the feeding of seagulls as in anything else. To the outsider it may seem a foolish and infantile hobby,
but it is clear that it must be a more prolific
field of experience than the outsider realises. I

[1] See *The Sporting Life,* by Robert Lynd. Grant Richards,
1922.

am only a beginner at it, but it seems to me already as though I had discovered an occupation that will leave me little time for anything else on Saturday and Sunday mornings. It is one of the few amusements that seem always to come to an end before one is tired. As you throw the last corner of the last slice of bread you have brought into the scramble of birds, you regret with a pang that you did not bring twice as much. You feel that you had only begun to enjoy yourself; besides, you feel that the birds are still as hungry as ever, if in fact they have not become even hungrier as a result of being fed. At least that is what I imagine you feel. I felt it by proxy as I watched the little girl searching for the ultimate crumb in the two corners of her paper bag. This may only have been the enthusiasm of an initiate: once I felt as enthusiastic about philology, about postage stamps, about hens. What child that has ever lived much on a farm believes that the interest of hens can ever come to an end? It is not merely that he can name the breed of every hen in the yard—Spanish, Leghorn, Dorking, Cochin China, Brahmaputra, Game, Bantam, Buff Orpington, and all the rest—but he knows the life, the habits and the appetites of each. He knows them as mothers; he knows which of them lays the most charming eggs; he knows which of them is the greediest and always arrives first with long, foolish strides beside the scattered banquet of mash. He knows the very chickens all but by name. He remembers the first effort of the young Dorking cockerel to crow like his father—a noise as though a gramophone gargled. He notices the ungainly, feathery legs of another overgrown cockerel, and, being reminded of a figure in the Scriptures, names him "Lazarus rising from the dead." He also knows every loose-liver in the yard—immoral hens that do not lay in the orthodox nests, but make nests of their own in the plantation across the road, or under a haystack or in a dark corner of the barn. Hens, indeed, are to him a crowded world, as some tribe of savages who would bore you and me are to an eager anthropologist. We may take it as certain that there is this infinite variety in any corner of life into which we peer with sufficient intensity of vision. The man of science looking through a microscope at a drop of water sees a world of living creatures of which the rest of us know nothing but by hearsay. If his microscope were strong enough, no doubt he would learn to distinguish each of these infinitesimal creatures from each other, and give each of them a separate name, as a farmer gives separate names to his cows. If his microscope

were stronger still, he might discover within one
of these infinitesimal creatures an apparently
infinite number of still tinier living creatures,
and so on, worlds without end.

Hence it seems reasonable to suppose that the
study of seagulls alone might keep a man interested and still making new discoveries for a
lifetime. At present I know nothing about them,
except that they have an endless appetite for
bread that even a restaurant proprietor would
shrink from putting into a cabinet pudding.
But I know enough to make me understand and
envy the people who stand on the Embankment
and on the bridges and bring a world of white
birds down about their heads to share their poor
luncheons. Some people love throwing things
to a dog—biscuits, lumps of sugar, etc.—but to
feed the seagulls is as good as throwing things
to many dogs.

Then there are ducks. The countryman may
boast of his nightingales, his larks, his wood-
peckers, his kingfishers, his jays. But, after all,
the ducks on the Serpentine have points of
superiority to any of these birds. They, too, will
repay you if you take your courage in both hands
and go out boldly with bread in a paper bag.
How nobly they ride the ripples of the stormy
pond, awaiting the bread-giver! How, on catch-

ing a distant sight of him, they hasten like a fleet
of small motor boats to his neighbourhood! How
exquisitely the blue feather shines out of the
drab in the wing even of the dullest duck! How
gorgeously the drake's head gleams with shift-
ing blue and green lights! How lordly his tail
curls! Was ever pig's tail prettier? Then there
are the tufted ducks, each with its straight back
hair blowing about in the wind like the straight
back hair of a quack dentist, or a piano-tuner, or
an elocution master. Each of them, too, has a
little round eye as yellow as bright sunshine, and
each of them has the gift of standing on its head
and performing feats as dexterous as the cart-
wheels of a street arab. I saw a small ragged boy
in Hyde Park last week amusing a baby in a per-
ambulator extemporised out of a sugar-box, by
throwing small stones among the tufted ducks.
I dislike the habit of throwing stones at ducks,
and, though none of them seemed to be hitting
the birds, I felt nervous for their little daffodil
eyes. I spoke my mind about it—not to the small
boy, for I am always afraid that if I reprove people my clerical blood may assert itself, but in an
aside to a lady. She went across to him, and
instead of treating him as a brand to be plucked
from the burning, as I should have done, she
spoke to him almost as a fellow-sinner. "You're

taking care not to hit any of them, aren't you?"
she said, beaming on him. He turned up a large
face on which there was a large smudge on each
cheek and a large smudge on his small nose.
He was just big enough to be able to walk and
talk without collapsing. He beamed good nature
and said in a series of gasps of excit ment:
"You throws things at 'em, and they stands on
their 'eads." It was certainly true. The tufted
ducks were standing on their heads peering
after the sunk pebbles in the hope that they
were bread, till they must have been giddy. As
I watched them my attitude to the youngster
changed. I, too, had rather see a duck standing
on its head than almost any other sort of acrobat. I love to see the uneasy equilibrium, and
the kicking legs with the joints going up and
down like piston-rods. Besides, it amused the
baby. Was it virtuous? I do not know. If one
of the ducks had been hit, my attitude would
probably have changed back again to the normal,
and I should have spoken my mind angrily—to
the lady. But no harm was done beyond giving
the ducks headaches. . . .

But the subject of ducks is endless. Have
you ever seen a teal? Why, a teal alone is the
beginning of a story as long as *The Arabian
Nights*.

# VIII

## GOOD LUCK

MANY people are complaining of a deluge of post cards that has lately fallen on England. Half the population seems already to have received them. They come to the just and the unjust, and no one can tell from whom, for they are all anonymous.

They are on an old pattern. When the world was more pious, post cards containing chain prayers used to be popular. Every one who received one of these post cards was expected to copy out the prayer on nine other post cards, and each of his victims was expected to copy the prayer out on nine other post cards in the hope that the prayer might ultimately make its way round the world. There was a theory that the repetition of a form of words would produce magical results. Most of the people who received these post cards were extremely annoyed by them. Many of them, however, would

sit down and write out their nine copies lest
something worse might befall them. It was
usually suggested that, if they did not do so,
they would be punished by some kind of ill luck,
and it is a poor spirit that will not purchase
immunity from ill luck at the cost of a few pence
and a little penmanship. Certainly, to break the
chain without consulting a clergyman would have
been to incur a grave responsibility.

The post card that is now going the rounds
of the world does not pretend to any religious
sanction. It simply expresses a wish for the re-
cipient's good luck. It runs as follows:—

"Good Luck! Copy this out and send it to nine
people to whom you wish good luck. The chain was
started by an American officer and should go around
the world eight times. Do not break the chain, as
whoever does will have bad luck. Do it within twenty-
four hours and count nine days and you will have
great good luck."

Now that on the surface is a very pretty kind
of wish. The prospect of having "great good
luck" as a result of merely writing nine post
cards and counting nine days is a far, far better
prospect than most of us have ever known. Yet it
is a curious fact that hardly anyone is grateful.

Good-tempered people may do little more than shrug their shoulders, but the plethoric and the peppery become unreasonably violent and talk as if they would be satisfied with nothing less than the American officer's blood. That American officer is just now the most unpopular man in England. He has committed the unpardonable sin of inventing a circular that cannot, unless you are inhumanly free from superstition, be thrown into the waste-paper basket without a second thought. How gentle in approach is the money-lender compared to him! Never a week passes but a money-lender offers to lend me from £5 to £5000—without security, God bless his trusting heart!—and never a threat does he utter, even by implication, if I do not respond in the same spirit. Yet, if he chose to employ threats, he could undoubtedly increase his business. If he wound up his circular with a hint that, if I did not borrow £5000, I should catch elephantiasis, I, for one, would be tempted to take his money and say no more about it. It is appalling to think of the vast sums one could be forced to borrow by these means. One would gradually find that one had become a millionaire through sheer timidity, and one would not like the responsibility of being a millionaire. A hundred thousand or so—one could at least spend that.

But it is difficult to see how one could spend a million pounds without impairing one's health. One would have to put it in a bank, and, if one put it in a bank, one might as well not have borrowed it. Luckily, the money-lender realises that he must not thrust his money on people who do not want it. If he did, he would become a social pest, and we should find a means of putting an end to his activities. As it is, one can throw his cards and his circulars into the waste-paper basket without a qualm. One even begins to think kindly of him as a possible friend in need.

It is otherwise with the sender of "good luck" post cards. If you receive one of them, your first thought is, "What enemy has done this?" You look for the signature, and find none. You look at the handwriting, and it is disguised. All that you know is that some wretched victim of superstition has attempted to ward off bad luck from himself by a cheap display of benevolence towards you. Sometimes it is cheap beyond forgiveness. I met a poet last week to whom someone had sent the "good luck" formula in an unstamped letter and who had to pay fourpence for the excess postage. It has had an extremely bad effect on him. He can think of nothing but revenge. Every day he decides on a different person as the one most likely to have wronged him, and no sooner does he do so than he dispatches his best wishes to them in an envelope without a stamp. Meanwhile the Post Office surplus mounts up. It is said that the Postmaster-General regards the American officer as the noblest figure that has appeared in America since Lincoln.

As for the rest of us, there is nothing to be gained from abusing the man. He has been loosed upon the world for some unknown reason, and we may as well make the best of him. After all there have been worse plagues in the past. There were the ten plagues of Egypt, and there was the Sphinx of Thebes. Any single one of the labours of Hercules was infinitely more exhausting than the filling up of nine post cards with a pretty little wish. The chief difficulty about the post cards is that one is reluctant to send them to the people to whom one really wishes good luck. It is not the sort of thing that one does to a friend. It is, I think, legitimate if the friend is an American, for, after all, America cannot get out of its responsibility for having produced the American officer. But it is not everyone who possesses nine American friends. In these circumstances, it is obvious that thousands of men and women must at present be

gravely perplexed as to what they ought to do.
I met a publisher who had received the post card
and who was in a state of great anxiety because
he felt that, if he did not send his nine post cards,
he would be taking risks that in the uncertain
state of the publishing world he could not afford
to take. I met a lady who was equally perturbed
as a result of receiving the post card, because
she wishes shortly to go to Paris by aeroplane.
These are but two representative figures in a
world of men and women who wish to behave
honourably and yet to behave in a way consistent
with safety. They cannot send post cards to
their friends—partly because, not being adept
forgers, they cannot disguise their handwriting
to a point at which a friend would not recognise
it—but they must send them to somebody.
Another lady with whom I discussed the problem
told me that she had got out of the difficulty in
a way which seems to me scarcely justifiable. At
first she had thought of sending all the nine post
cards to dignitaries of the Church. She had just
decided to address one to Dean Inge when suddenly there appeared in her mind a pathetic
vision of that austere preacher sitting down,
wrapped in deeper gloom than ever, and more in
sorrow than in anger, to copy out his toll of
post cards. Not only this, but she felt sure that

scores of his admirers had sent the Dean the post
card already.  Every morning's post must bring
at least a dozen, and, as each of them has to be
copied out nine times, she saw him in her mind's
eye toiling in secret and without intermission at
his endless stream of post cards, stretching his
thumb at intervals to keep off writer's cramp,
with groanings unutterable.  Who in the circumstances could have added to his burden?
Not, at least, this lady, of all ladies the most
charitable.

She consequently turned for help to the London Telephone Directory and picked out nine
names from it more or less at random.  She
chose them, she said, for their beauty.  She
thought at first of sending some of the cards to
limited liability companies the names of which
specially attracted her.  There was the Jiffy
Prepared Firewood Co., for instance, and there
was Jigs, Ltd., Engineering Tools Designers.
Then there was another curious company that
had only initials and was entered in the Directory
as J. M., Shock Absorbers Works.  It is a question that calls for the subtlety of a mediæval
schoolman, however—whether to wish good luck
to a limited liability company is the same thing
as to wish good luck to a person.  The lady wisely
decided not to risk it.  She accordingly limited

her choice to the names of individual men and
women. She sent the first card to a fish salesman
with a delightful name who had an address in
Billingsgate Buildings. She was tempted at first
to send the whole nine to fish salesmen. It was
pleasant to imagine the sort of things a fish salesman belonging to Billingsgate Buildings would
say on looking through his morning post and discovering the peccant post card. It is doubtful
whether anybody but a fish salesman, indeed,
could do justice to the situation. It seemed unfair, however, to upset the fish market on the
eve of Holy Week—especially unfair to provoke
it to speech scarcely congruous with the Lenten
season. She therefore resolved not to send more
than one card to men who had the same profession. She addressed the second card to an um-
brella manufacturer at Hornsey, the third to a
toy-dog breeder, the fourth to a hatter in order
to make him madder still, the fifth to a man who
was described as a "Whsle Frntre Mnfr," and
who is therefore probably Welsh, the sixth to a
Scottish humorist in order to give him something
to make him laugh on the wrong side of his
mouth, the seventh to a Presbyterian minister,
the eighth to a turf accountant, and the ninth to
a potato merchant with what she called a "perfectly heavenly name." By this time she had

begun thoroughly to enjoy herself, and, when
she had written the ninth address, she felt something akin to the deep regret with which Gibbon
laid down his pen as he finished *The Decline and
Fall of the Roman Empire.* One has only to
turn to the Telephone Directory and dip casually
among the names and professions that are mentioned in it in order to realise how much she must
have enjoyed herself. No novelist dare invent
such names as appear in profusion in that admirable volume. The names in Dickens and Meredith are tame compared to some of them. At the
same time, it is a question whether it is not
malicious to wish a man good luck merely because he has a beautiful name. The lady is now
counting the nine days carefully to see whether
the spell works in such unusual circumstances.
As the ninth day approaches, she is beginning to
wish that, after all, she had sent the post cards to
her friends. She declares that she does honestly
wish the best of luck to the fish salesman and the
toy-dog breeder and the turf accountant and the
Presbyterian minister. But can one be said to
wish good luck to a person of whom one knows
nothing but his profession and his name? It is to
be hoped that one can, as one is glad to think of
what the Scottish humorist said about the American officer when he went out to buy a packet of

post cards. I do not think he said a word in excess of what the situation required. I received one of the post cards myself, and I have no doubt he expressed my feelings exactly.

# IX

## FEBRUARY

IF tradition is to be relied on, all the birds that are not already married choose their mates on St. Valentine's Day. Some recent ornithologists dispute this old country belief, but there is evidence for it in the poets, who, after all, know as much about nature as most people. Donne wrote more than three hundred years ago:

> Hail, Bishop Valentine, whose day this is;
> All the air is thy diocese,
> And all the chirping choristers
> And other birds are thy parishioners:
> Thou marriest every year
> The lyric lark and the grave whispering dove,
> The sparrow that neglects his life for love,
> The household bird with the red stomacher;
> Thou mak'st the blackbird speed as soon
> As doth the goldfinch or the halcyon.

If anything, the birds have anticipated St. Valentine's Day this year. The hedge-sparrows

have been singing their quick little stumbling
line for some days past and have been eyeing
one another critically with lowered heads in the
branches.  It has been an early year for many
things.  The larks at the foot of the hills were
springing into the air, jerkily as little boys that
are learning to swim, a fortnight ago, and singing above ash-buds black in the frost of January.
On a wet Sunday afternoon—wet enough to
frighten cats from coming out and so to make
the world safe for thrushes—hill-sides, valleys
and gardens were all busy with choirs shouting
against each other in rehearsal for the spring.
The thrush, the robin and the wren all seemed
to rejoice in the wetness, as though their very
songs were sweeter for the rain.  Crows, too,
have been practising their seven caws in the fields
in preparation for family life in the tree-tops.
What it is that the crows talk about is a secret
from most of us.  One fancies that many of
them are jokers much given to pulling other
crows' legs.  Seldom are they settled in a field
for long when one of them suddenly gives warning, like the boy crying "Nix!" and startles the
whole crowd of them into circles of flight. They
settle down again, a whirl of them coming to
rest, and again a rook gives the alarm.  Off they
are, the more nervous of them, on short circling

flights, and, if you watch them for an hour, you will not often see them at rest for more than a few seconds at a time. It may be that you can fool all of the crows some of the time and some of the crows all of the time, but that you cannot fool all of the crows all of the time. One cannot tell. What seems probable, however, is that many of the crows enjoy being jostled into fear. They want an excuse for movement: that is apparently the origin of most games. To keep perpetually moving is a Law of Nature with them as it is with flies and planets. The ability to move at will is the chief thing that distinguishes a living creature from a stone. Hence living creatures abhor stillness and stagnation as properties of the dead. Children, birds and fish are seldom still. They must circulate at all costs —not for any purpose, save that circulation is a good thing in itself. The mystics tell us that, though the life of the animal is to be found in movement, the life of the spirit is to be found in stillness. Luckily for themselves, the rooks are not faced with the difficulty of choosing between the life of the animal and the life of the spirit. Luckily for us, we are. But even we, whatever our choice, must spend a considerable part of our lives going into town and coming out again, going to the post and coming

back again, going upstairs and coming down
again. While we do these things for the sake of
making a living, we persuade ourselves that we
are usefully employed. But, even if we had not
to make a living, we should spend a great part of
our lives in comings and goings, in unsettlings
and settlings, very much like the crows. A man
must live, and life consists in hurrying from one
place to another, from one person to another,
from one thing to another.

There are times when we could wish it were
otherwise—when we would welcome an enchanter
who with a touch of his wand would bid everything stand still and remain as it is, as in the
palace of the Sleeping Beauty. Even the palace
of the Sleeping Beauty, however, would hardly
satisfy us. We wish to have the stillness of
perfect life, not the stillness of death or of death-
like sleep. We long for a world that shall reach
perfection and remain perfect and unchangeable
for ever, like a lyric of Shakespeare. Our sense
of fact may forbid us actually to picture such a
world as something to be desired, but our longing for it is shown in the regret with which a
child bids good-bye to a summer holiday—a regret that repeats itself all through our lives.
Looking back, we may find it difficult to say:
"There—or there—life should have stood still

and remained unchanged for ever." We may wish present happiness to last for ever: we seldom wish that past happiness had lasted for ever. If we feel the wish that we could live our lives over again, we do not wish merely for the return of one experience, but for the return of a whole series of experiences. Even when we long for the extension of present happiness, it may be that we should feel alarmed if we were suddenly told that it was going to last, immutable, for ever. We desire a prolonged time, rather than an eternity, of most kinds of happiness.

> Would that I
> Might see three springs without a break go by.

More than this might well prove a surfeit. As a matter of fact, we like the months to circulate like the planets and the crows. A spring that lasted too long would set most of us dreaming of the fruits of summer and the colours of autumn, as a summer that lasted too long would set us dreaming of the snows of winter. Things are much better as they are. This is not Heaven that it can do without the procession of day and night, of heat and cold, and of the four seasons. And even in the Heaven that men have pictured, the angels do not stand still, but circulate like the stars or like birds. Perfect stillness and

perfect silence would not be Paradise. In any
case, if we were miraculously given the power
to pick out any one season of the year, and to
command it, "Remain like this for ever," it is
unlikely that one human being in a million would
choose February for the experiment. February
is, at best, only a beginning—the first stammer-
ing of spring. Even the thrushes' songs are not
what they will be in April. Every voice in the
trees is a prophecy of something still more delightful. It is a promise, like the brown or red
or green or black buds. Is there anything in
Nature that is lovelier in February than in any
other month of the year? I doubt if a single
thing could be named of which this could be said.
The hazels, perhaps, with their green catkins
hanging, like a suspended shower, in their bare
branches; but there is nothing else that will not
be better in March.

There is one thing, however, that most of us
wish might circulate less in February. We do
not complain if the air is still. Winter air is
one of the things that can be still without being
stagnant. As a matter of fact, the stiller it is
the more it seems to tingle with life. It is not
the leaden-coloured wind from the east that
makes the island seem to spring to life in
February. The whole planet lies numb under its

baleful breath. Every tree grows skeleton-like,
and every bird silent at its approach; the pulse
beats feebly, the brain retreats as into a cave.
Compare with it a brisk, still morning. The
beech, with its long, lean buds seems to spring
from the ground like a fire. It is a fire with the
play of countless tiny fires among its branches.
The elm, which is a plume in shape, is flushed in
its highest branches with the first tide of blossom.
Everywhere the spring seems like a runner
stooping in readiness for the signal to start. For
weeks past little pink tips have been catching
the sunlight for the earliest buds. Most of the
birds, it is true, still move about in congrega-
tions. A troupe of long-tailed tits crosses from
plantation to plantation, swimming through the
air like a shoal of fishes, or rather like a procession of fishes, one waiting to start until the other
has arrived; each of them rising and falling in a
flight like the curve of a wave. Having arrived
in the tops of the beeches, they become acrobats,
flinging themselves from peril to peril in an endless trapeze act, encouraging each other in voices
as tiny as the voice of a coal-tit, as tiny almost
as the voice of the goldcrest. They are colour-
less, except when they cross the sun; all small
birds are mice in the chill February light. In
the bright sun they may become dyed in colour,

just as a crow wheeling in the light may momentarily become a flash of gold or a gleam of purple. A chaffinch in the sunlight may bring the colours of Arabia into a cart-wheel track in a lane.

But February is nothing to what March will be—less than nothing to what April will be. If one had to hibernate for a month in the year, this is the month one would choose. We say of any unpleasant period in public affairs that it is a period of transition. It is a phrase we never use of a time we wish to praise. Every year in history was a year of transition, but we never say so unless there is nothing good to say about it. It is the excuse, we make for bad times—a hopeful excuse, for it implies that something better must follow. February might justly be described as a month of transition.

And yet to call February a month of transition seems a grudging way in which to speak of the first month of lovers. After all, St. Valentine's Day must once have had a meaning, and even to-day it survives as an occasion for jest among boys and girls in the less haughty classes. They say that, though Valentine was a saint, no church was ever dedicated to him, yet to most of us he is a more familiar figure than, say, St. Botolph. Is it not in his honour that servant-girls post the tails of salted herrings to their lovers—good sport, that puts no strain on the intellect? St. Valentine's Day is, or used to be, the great day for anonymous letters. It was almost the only occasion on which a human being could write an anonymous letter without being a half-wit or a scoundrel. It was the day of the comedy of love —of Cupid the leg-puller. The youth who opens a Valentine on St. Valentine's morning is less likely to receive a confession of love than a portrait of a blinking idiot. It is said that the day was once taken more seriously, but after all, who could take even love seriously in February? Valentines are but a playful anticipation, as the whole month at its best is a playful anticipation of a real spring. The truth is, St. Valentine was the patron saint, not of the lover, but of the flirt. It is possible that chaffinches regard him as the god of love, but among human beings his altar has long been cold. He should have chosen a different day. Had his feast day been the first of April he would have been immortal.

# X

## BEAVER

NOTHING could more effectively demonstrate the confused state of the civilised world than the fact that while the inhabitants of England are playing (or supposed to be playing) Beaver, the male inhabitants of Sacramento were ordered a few months ago to grow beards on pain of being fined half-a-dollar a day. Thus are beards turned into sport in one patch of the planet while they are publicly reverenced in another. In this respect the people of Sacramento rather than the people of England are followers of the ancient tradition. To play Beaver is to put oneself on a level with the children who cried, "Go up, thou baldhead!" to Elisha, for to laugh at a superfluity of hairs on the chin is as bad as to laugh at the want of them on the top of the head. Apart from this, a nation that owes so much to the Old Testament as the English should treat beards with respect. The Jew has always put beards in their right place, which is on human

chins. Right through the centuries eminent
Jews have held that to remove the beard was a
sin, seeing that God originally gave man a beard
in order to distinguish him from woman; and to
neglect one's beard in Old Testament times was
regarded as a sign of madness. Heretics again
and again revolted in favour of the clip or the
clean shave, but the Cabalists returned to sanity
with the proclamation that even to shorten the
beard with scissors was a great sin, and it was
said of their master, Isaac Luria, that so scrupu-
lous was his guardianship of his beard that he
would not touch it with his hands "lest the con-
tact should cause any hairs to drop from it."
Judaism was again and again cloven asunder
by the dispute about beards. One ribald anti-
Beaver summed up the case against beards in the
epigram:

If men be judged wise by their beards and their girth,
Then goats were the wisest of creatures on earth.

Which is not even true.

*The Jewish Encyclopædia* tells us that in the
seventeenth century the Jews in Germany and
Italy began to circumvent the prohibition of
shaving by "removing the beard by means of
pumice-stone or chemical agents, which left the
face smooth as if shaven." Since that time the

Jewish laity seem to have become more and more lax in regard to the growing of beards. We can hardly blame them if the Talmudical saying which suggests that a man's character is given away by his beard is true. "A thin-bearded man is cunning," says the proverb, "a thick-bearded one is a fool; but nobody can do any harm to a man with a parted beard." It is better to shave than to risk not having a parted beard.

Christians, unfortunately, have been divided even more bitterly than the Jews on the question of beards. It was "one of the great subjects of reproach" on the part of the Greek Church, we are told, that the Romish clergy did not let their beards grow, though a leading theologian pointed out that it was absurd to get excited over a matter that had as little to do with salvation as *barbæ detonsio aut conservatio.* Rome, however, was so vehemently opposed to the wearing of beards that in 1119 clergy who let their hair and beards grow were threatened with excommunication, while the mystically-minded Durandus explained, according to *The Catholic Encyclopædia,* that "length of hair is symbolical of the multitude of sins. Hence clerics are directed to shave their beards; for the cutting of the hair of the beard, which is said to be nourished by the superfluous humours of the stomach, denotes

that we ought to cut away the vices of sins which
are a superfluous growth in us. Hence we shave
our beards that we may seem purified by innocence and humility, and that we may be like the
angels who remain always in the bloom of
youth." At the same time, the instinct for
growing beards remained so strong that several
of the Popes themselves succumbed to it, and
even as recently as 1865 the Pope was forced to
reprimand certain of the clergy of Bavaria for
attempting to re-introduce the fashion of wearing beards. He is said to have rebuked them in
the words, *"Non Beaveria sed Bavaria,"* but this
may not be true.

England, above all other nations, should be
slow to speak disrespectfully of beards. The
greatest age of English history was an age of
beards. In the spacious days of Elizabeth the
beards were as spacious as the days. Shakespeare wore a beard, and, if he were alive to-day,
undergraduates on holiday would be looking
over his garden wall at Stratford and shouting
"Beaver!" Had not one of the Queen's agents
abroad a beard five feet long? Yet so degener-
ate had England become by the end of the eight-
eenth century that Lord Rokeby's growing a
beard was regarded as evidence that he was mad,
and it was said that he was the only peer in the

country who did not shave. In the nineteenth century a revival of literature was followed by a revival of beards, and the reign of Queen Victoria was as prolific of bearded men of letters and bearded artists as the reign of Queen Elizabeth had been. It is strange that queens and beards should thus go together. Queen Anne alone seems to have ruled over men of genius who grew no beards. It would be worth some statistician's while to go through the great names of English literature and compare the amount of genius that has gone bearded with the amount of genius that has been clean-shaven. The beardless, I fancy, would be in a numerical majority, but we can estimate the weight of genius on the other side when we remember that Chaucer, Shakespeare, Bacon, Spenser, Dickens, Carlyle, Ruskin, Browning, Tennyson, Swinburne, Meredith, Morris and Mr. Shaw have all worn beards, while Matthew Arnold wore whiskers. The great ages of prose are the ages in which men shave. The great ages of poetry are those in which they allow their beards to grow. Thus, as we should have expected, the lawyers, who are of all men the most prosaic, are the least given to wearing beards. It was even a rule of the society of Lincoln's Inn for a time in the sixteenth century that anyone who appeared at their mess wearing a beard should be fined and expelled. How many barristers are there to-day who would dare to assume either the prophet's or the poet's beard?

One is amazed at the vanity of human beings who will thus expose their features to the general view when nature has provided so easy a means of disguising them. It is not even that they get any pleasure from shaving. There is no operation more tedious, quite apart from the danger of being infected with anthrax from the shaving-brush. As for being shaved by a barber, that, too, has its perils. I remember being shaved during a thunderstorm by a little French barber who leaped into the air at every flash of lightning, and brought the razor back to my throat like a guillotine in his unsteady hand. On another occasion the barber was tipsy, and by the time he had covered all one side of my face with duelling-marks I had to beg him to desist, and went out into the world shaven (more or less) on the right side of the face, and with a stubble of beard on the left. It is strange what perils men will face merely in order not to look different from their neighbours. It may be that most men do not care how they look, so long as they do not look ridiculous, and their conception of looking ridiculous is that they should look dif-

ferent from anybody else.  It is less than a century since an English painter was driven into
writing a pamphlet in defence of his beard.  The
convention of one age is the laughing-stock of
the next.  In regard to shaving, the view of the
conventionalist is that it does not much matter
whether we shave or grow beards provided we
all shave or grow beards at the same time, and
ninety-nine men out of a hundred are con-
ventionalists.

Despite all the perils of the shaving-brush, and
the still greater perils of the barber's shop, it
seems to me likely that Englishmen will continue
to shave till a queen sits on the throne again.
They will shave in greater numbers than ever, as
soon as the game of Beaver passes out of the
comparatively narrow circle of university men
and spreads to taxi-drivers, bus-conductors and
newsboys.  Life will become intolerable for a
bearded man when children rise up out of the
pavement at every step and surround him with
loud shouts of "Beaver!"  Anyone who has ever
worn his hair half-an-inch longer than a Christian
should must remember how even the emptiest
street could echo, as with the horns of elfland
faintly blowing, with the silver whistled notes
that represent "Get your hair cut!"  The English are supposed to be individualists, but they

are not individualists when it comes to growing
long hair or a beard. The universal whistling of
"Get your hair cut!" was one of the minor perse-
cutions of the nineteenth century. You could
enjoy being whistled at only if you had a taste
for being a minor martyr. As a good many
young men had, as a matter of fact, grown their
hair long in a spirit of challenge, they got a certain amount of amusement from the whistlings
of draymen and bus-drivers. Men do not, however, grow beards as a challenge. They grow
them, as a rule, for purposes of concealment, and,
when their efforts at concealment only serve to
bring them into the limelight, they will be compelled either to emigrate to a free country or to
retire into the obscurity of a clean shave.

It is to be hoped that some expert will leave
for future generations a record of the rules of
the game of Beaver. It is played, I understand,
by two persons, and the points are scored as in
tennis. Whichever of the two first cries
"Beaver!" as a beard heaves into sight, scores.
At sight of a white beard, one cries, "Polar
beaver!" which counts a game. At sight of a
royal beard, the correct call is "Royal beaver!"
which counts not only as game, but as sett and
match. There is a story of a Cambridge function
at which, on the entrance of King George V.,

the audience of undergraduates rose to their feet
with a universal shout of "Royal beaver! Game,
sett, match!" It is possibly untrue. There are,
I believe, still other variations of the game, and,
no doubt, in time it will become as elaborate in
its niceties as poker. Whatever its future, however, I feel sure that it will remain a purely
English game. It is a game that could only be
played by a race of men who can keep their faces
straight. Foreigners are too excitable. They
would come to blows. Beards would be plucked,
and hair pulled in revenge. Englishmen can
play the game, however, with calm faces and
without moving a muscle even in a smile. The
bearded man knows that he is under observation,
but so guileless, so impassive, are the faces of
those whom he meets that he never knows by
whom he is being observed. He feels as if he
were being shadowed by a secret society, so
polite, so grave, is every face he sees. Beaver,
indeed, is the most secret of games. So quietly
is it played that thousands of Londoners have
never once heard the cry of "Beaver!" in a public
place, though the game may be in progress all
round them. It is said to be in full swing at
Church Parade on Sundays, but if you mix in the
crowd at Church Parade you will listen for even
a whisper of the word in vain.

Elderly people say that is a silly game, and
that is true enough. On the other hand, it is a
silly game in the English tradition of silliness.
Swift and Harley, when driving out together,
used to play a similar game with cats. The first
of them who saw a cat and cried, "There's a
cat!" scored. It may be that all games are silly.
But, then, so are human beings. This does not
happen to be the planet into which the wiser
spirits choose to be born.

# XI

## KNEE-DEEP IN JUNE

OFFICIALLY, there is a drought. A drought is what you and I would call a spell of fine weather. The Meteorological Office apparently defines it as a spell of fine weather that lasts without a break for a fortnight.

But the farmers, as well as the Meteorological Office are saying that there is a drought. "I have had that field ploughed four times," declared Mr. Finch, nodding over the hedge at three acres of broken soil; "I want to get on with my swedes, but it's no use till it rains." Happy are we to whom swedes mean less than sunshine. We have no more complaint to make of the warm air than has the Painted Lady that spreads her dappled fans to the sun on the broad green hazel-leaf. We have no more complaint to make than has the happy-ash tree in the paddock, swaying the burden of its leaves in the bright wind as though it too had some impulse of wings. There is a plenitude of satisfaction in the world at this

season—a lushness of life that more than com-
pensates for the lost blossom of the apple-tree
and the fading of the chestnut blossom into the
unsightliness of a thaw. The very grass is full of
colours. As you lie in it, a neglected book in
your pocket, it seems to tremble with a dust of
blue flowers in the summer light. Only one
sort of grass, perhaps, and the flowers, when you
look at them closer, are slate-grey. And what a
tribe of insects is flying and flitting and creeping
among the blades! There is one creature, who
looks like a flying earwig, his head and tail of
the colour of raw bacon, and who hastens from
blade to blade on an interminable quest. He
begins near the ground and creeps up the grass
till, when he has reached the top, it bends under
his weight and suspends him perilously over the
abyss. At times he struggles to right himself,
and wrestles with the blade as with an enemy.
But in the end he opens his wing-cases and flies
off hopefully, his tail low like a weight carried
by a pulley, to climb another blade. He does
this an infinite number of times. He never tires;
he never despairs; perhaps he never thinks. Is
he a beast of prey, sating his appetite all the
while on an innocent and frightened population?
Is he in pursuit of infinitesimal creatures to
whom the grass is a branching forest and whose

sky is no higher than the hedge of the field? It
may be that he is not half so monstrous in his
appetites as that small, quiet moth on a grass-
stem near him, with folded wings that are shaped
like the roof of a Noah's Ark and brocaded like
a teal. The moth is watchful and still. He does
not fuss upon his errand. He is quiet as a flower.
Even when he flies, he flies on soft wings, dodg-
ing the grasses as a bird dodges the stems of
trees.

Towards evening a little grey moth, its wings
grained like a shell, comes in its scores and
flutters through the nettles and the grasses. But
in the sunlight the congregation of the flies and
the butterflies is more noticeable. The Orange-
Tip is everywhere, with an island mapped on his
white wing. The Cabbage-White lurches over
the hedge, and bolts up the paddock as though
tumbling over itself in its haste. We are accustomed to think of the butterfly as a wayward
creature of indeterminate flight, but never did
fugitive make greater haste or with firmer purpose than that Cabbage-White as it fled along the
hedge from its imaginary pursuer. I do not
know whether there are any statistics in regard
to the speed of butterflies, but here, at least, was
one that would have left a pursuing entomologist
breathless. Then there was a smaller white

butterfly—a charming marbled creature with
black veins and a hint of green. But he, alas!
could not fly. He could but flutter a few yards,
and then sink on the ground, and roll over, like
a fishing-smack when the tide has retreated. It
may be that he was a baby, learning to crawl in
the air. Or it may be that he was crippled, and
would flop uneasily about the earth till a sparrow
made a meal of him. A more humane man than
I might have given him the benefit of the doubt
and put him out of his misery. I left him, however, to his share of a world that vibrated with
the wings of Orange-Tips and Fritillaries. Let
the sparrows be his executioners if they would.

In the hedge round the paddock a whitethroat
is noisy all day. He is a delightful little creature,
with a song like a signature scribbled with a quill
pen. He keeps out of sight most of the time,
but he cannot resist the temptation of an occasional upward dive into the air, as though he
were playing at being a lark. He even attempts
to imitate the lark's profuseness of speech when
on the wing, as he jerks and scrambles and side-
slips among the air above the trees. Then suddenly he becomes frightened and precipitates
himself downwards in a series of desperate dives
till he has reached the safety of the hedge or his
post in an ash-tree again. This, I think, is a

whitethroat year. Or perhaps Mr. Finch's farm
is a specially favoured haunt of whitethroats.
Every lane and every field is full of them. They
are more conspicuous than the chaffinches. No
wonder that the wren, sitting on the barn, has to
sing like a Wagnerian tenor pitting himself
against the orchestra. He would not be heard
otherwise. No wonder that when I awoke in the
darkness before the dawn I heard the lark singing—filling the night with music that, at that
hour, seemed ghostly, unearthly, like the voices
of adoring spirits. He, too, had no other chance
of being heard. Shortly after him came the
cuckoo, his voice already becoming a stammer.
Or he may have been a young bird, having his
first lessons from a terrifying singing-master.
But there was a long silence between the lark's
first silvering of the darkness and the full chorus
of the trees and hedges, with blackbirds dominating the world with their grave recitations. There
are in this part of the country twenty blackbirds
or more to every thrush. The first hour of morning is a blackbirds' service. There is one blackbird who intones, and all the other blackbirds
make the responses. As things work out, it is a
little more confused than that. The blackbirds
interrupt one another, and, if you listen closely,
you will perceive that each of them is asking

questions. The first blackbird asks a question, and, before he has finished, a blackbird in a neighbouring tree is replying to him by asking another question. And so the interrogation passes from tree to tree, from parish to parish, from county to county, to the extreme limit of the world at which a blackbird can be found. So far as I know, the question has never been answered. I do not even know what the question is. But it begins afresh every morning, as though it were something radiantly novel and undebated, like the "Why?" and the "Whence?" and the "Whither?" that we poor creatures who haven't even wings have been putting for ten thousand years to the perfectly charming and perfectly silent stars. Alas, the blackbirds are up a tree, and so are we. But with what suavity, with what dulcet dignity, they continue the eternal discussion!

The blackcap is another matter. I did not see him, but I heard him in a nettle-grown dell fifty yards from the house, singing in an ash-tree from which I had seen dead stoats hanging two months before. He puts no questions. His sole business is to escape from harshness into music. The blackcap begins his song as though he were utterly incapable of music. He is harsh, husky, scratchy. He, too, writes with a quill pen.

Gradually all this changes. A note that begins as a creak ends as pure music. It is as though a freed spirit sang above the prison of the body —as though the sun had been released, round and gold, from its birth among ragged clouds. Notes scarcely less lovely than a nightingale's fill the wood—note hastily on the heels of note, as though the bird were aware that its music could not last but might at any moment sink back again behind the ragged clouds. Perhaps the very insecurity of the song makes the sweetness all the more penetrating.

But the most fascinating of the birds in the neighbourhood is not a song-bird but the little owl—that small wild cat of the air that has been spreading so disastrously through England since its introduction by a well-meaning peer a generation or so ago. There are two little owls' nests in the paddock. One of them is in a hollow pear-tree to the east; and the other is in a hollow apple-tree to the west. The little owl is not a nightbird to anything like the same extent as the other owls. It flies furtively from tree to tree, wicked in the full blaze of the sun. It has a guilty conscience and glides down in the shadow of the trees on noiseless wings at the slightest movement. Before dipping into the hole of the tree that is its house, it takes up a position in the

crook of a low branch and looks round to see if
it is being observed. It sits infamously still, and,
standing in the darkness of a barn door, you can
see the yellow of its eyes twenty yards away. At
intervals it jerks nervously round, like a criminal
expecting the hand of a detective on his shoulder.
Should it see you, and should you not move, it
begins to bob its body up and down at you, as
though to say, "If you are alive, go away!"
There is a scene in *The Kid* in which Charlie
Chaplin bobs his body up and down in the same
threatening way every time his runaway enemy
looks round. His every gesture was an intima-
tion that he would be after the fellow if he did
not clear off in double-quick time. But everybody knew that Charlie himself would have run
for his life if the man had but turned and come
towards him. The owl was like that. A little
girl in a blue overall said to me: "Let us bob at
him and see what he will do." She bobbed in
imitation of him. He bobbed again. She bobbed
in answer. He did not wait for any more of it,
but fled like a guilty soul right out of the paddock. We went over to look into his nest where
three little white downy creatures slept, with
their beaks over each other's necks, blissful and
innocent as tiny pigs. You could see them either
by looking down into the hollow stem of the tree

from above, or by looking through the small hole in the side out of which the owl swept the garbage of beetles' wing-cases and other uneatable things, as down a rubbish-chute. There were no other comforts or conveniences in the home. Near the three little pigs lay the dried skin of a mouse, eaten long before the nestlings were out of the shell. As for the nestlings themselves, innocent though they at first appeared, each had already the Roman nose of its father and mother; and one wondered whether, in fairness to the other birds, they ought ever to have been allowed to leave the shell. One egg still lay in the nest unhatched. It was a nice case of conscience whether to take it away or leave it to its small chance of bursting into a bird of prey. If you have heard the other birds clamouring over the safety of their infants when an owl is watching them from a tree, you do not want to see too many owls—not, at least, too many little owls, who are but predatory aliens—in the world. The worst of it was, when we had taken the egg, we ceased to be certain that it was an owl's egg. An owl's egg, I believe, is perfectly white: this was spotted with brown. An owl's egg, I believe, is perfectly round: this, though almost round, was inclined to oval. It raised problems for the intellect as well as for the conscience.

In order to keep from thinking about it we went down the road and gathered hardheads and sat down on a bank of vetches and played the first three rounds of the hardhead championship of Hertfordshire. I was accused of cheating because I made rules, as anyone might have done, which enabled me to win handsomely. But I am rather clever at hardheads. It is a good game, and I have only one fault to find with it: it is too strenuous for a summer game. The muscles of my right arm are still a little stiff from it. But, at least, I won the championship. If I had gone to Oxford or Cambridge, I should almost certainly have got a Blue for hardheads.

# XII

## DRESSES

THOUSANDS of the most earnest minds in the kingdom, all of them female, look to Ascot every year for guidance. This year they looked to it finally to confirm their faith in the triumph of the long skirt and the large hat. This is not the unimportant matter it seems to grave persons. The fate of kingdoms has depended on more trifling things. A large hat may make all the difference to a modern Cleopatra in ensnaring a modern Mark Antony (in a white topper), and the course of civilisation may be diverted as a result. There is no doubt that it is easier to fall in love in some years than in others, and this is almost entirely due to the fashions of the day. It is at least twice as easy to fall in love in a year of long skirts as in a year of short, and in a year of large hats as in a year of small. Love with the ordinary human being is a perfectly superficial emotion, and, if the novelists were true to life, they would write less

about hearts and more about dresses.  There is
a great deal of nonsense written in the tradition
of King Cophetua and the beggar maid.  That
irregular love affairs of the kind have occurred
is true, but they are rare.  Generally speaking,
we may say that whether King Cophetua falls in
love or not depends on how the lady is dressed.
I do not say this cynically: I believe it to be
partly true.  I doubt if women would go to all
this trouble of dressing up if they, too, did not
believe that a perfect woman nobly planned is
the result of a collaboration between the Al-
mighty and a dressmaker.  Joan of Arc may be
different; St. Catherine of Siena may be different; I am speaking merely of the perfect
heroine of the average monarch or the average
man.  Women sometimes indignantly deny that
they dress for the eyes of men.  They dress, they
say, to please themselves, and are more interested in what women think than in what men
think about their clothes.  We must not dismiss
this too summarily as a feminine falsehood.  New
pleasures have undoubtedly arisen in the course
of the evolution of women's dress, and these
derivative pleasures have probably become the
chief pleasures of many well-dressed women.
Dress, like poetry, began as an art with a purpose.  It has evolved into an art for art's sake.

Hence modern women will discuss each other's dresses in much the same spirit in which Georgian poets discuss each other's poems. They are artists, and they know, like all artists, that their most sympathetic audience is one of women. They are no more concerned with the origins of dress than a poet is with the origins of verse. They have reached a point at which they enjoy being beautiful—at which, indeed, they could not help being beautiful—for its own sake. As a matter of fact, the modern woman who has not at least the air of dressing like a disinterested artist is not well dressed. Almost any woman can dress well enough to attract the admiration of a man; it is the test of a well-dressed woman that she can attract the admiration of other women.

Certainly, women would have a poor time of it if they had to depend on men for intelligent appreciation of their clothes. Men are influenced by women's clothes as they are influenced by the architecture of churches, but the influence in both cases is hypnotic: it does not awaken the observation and intelligence, but overwhelms them. Only a man of the worst sort, on returning from a party, could tell you how the women to whom he talked were dressed. Men get little more than a vague impression of colour, if they get as

much as that. I remember hearing of a young
reporter who was once sent to describe an important wedding in a small provincial town. His
brain swam as he looked round him, reflecting
that it was part of a duty to take back a detailed
account of the women's dresses. In despair he
appealed to a lady, who was describing the wedding for the rival local journal. She was an
extremely wicked lady who saw an opportunity
for an unpardonable joke. She knew all about
cookery in the original French, and she poured
into the boy's eager ear the most extraordinary
list of words it had ever been his lot to hear. She
robed all the guests in *soufflées* and *salmis* and
*vol-au-vents*. She trimmed the bride's mother's
dress with *petits fours* and the bride's aunt's hat
with *épinards*. She made everybody present
perfectly eatable, whether as a soup, an entrée
or a sweet. She made the bridegroom wear
some kind of jam in his buttonhole, and she
shod the bridesmaids in vegetables. There has, I
believe, never been quite so wonderful a description of a wedding anywhere else in English jour-
nalism. And it got into print simply because
there was nobody but men in the office of the
paper. The sub-editors were men; the printers
were men; and both were content to pass any
description of women's dress as something so

utterly beyond the masculine intelligence that they did not even think of asking whether it meant anything. They knew that clothes, like music, were talked about in a jargon, and they were humble men who regarded such things as beyond their comprehension. We may fancy that, had we been in control, we should never have allowed such a hoax to pass. But let us not be too sure. We are not sufficiently interested in such things to see when a writer on them is mistaken. We appreciate to some extent the ultimate effect of dress, but we are utterly bored by the technique of dress. A man may cast his eye lightly down a column about women's fashions, but, if he has a sound mind in a sound body, he cannot read it with the close attention and understanding with which he reads a column about finance or racing. His own art of dress and woman's art of dress are poles asunder. Man aims at protective colouring in his clothes, woman at attractive colouring. Man wears a costume in order to hide, woman in order to shine. "Man," somebody has said, "is a poem pretending to be a formula; woman is a formula pretending to be a poem." This, of course, is rubbish, as are most of the things we say about the sexes. But we may concede that there is a grain of sense in it, in so far as man dresses

in order to be inconspicuous while this can hardly
be said of women. This, we may admit, is only
natural. Men are unpleasant-looking creatures.
They have hairy faces and long feet. The average male European is not a person with whom
even a dressmaker of genius could do anything.
Hence his scorn of dress. Hence his attempt
to conceal his identity in a dark suit and a bowler
hat. Artists are constantly resurrecting the
theory that the male form is more beautiful than
the female. There is no arbiter for such an argument. Women may at least claim that the picture papers are on their side. There is little to
be said for photographs of either sex on the score
of beauty, but it can hardly be questioned that
the portraits of men who get into the public
eye are much more repulsive than the portraits
of any of the women.

On the whole, the world has never done justice
to women's clothes. When they are mentioned
in literature, it is usually with sarcasm or de-
nunciation. The prophets and satirists have said
more about them than have the lyric poets. True,
there are charming pieces in praise of dress, such
as Herrick's: "When as in silks my Julia goes."
But in the higher sort of poetry little is made
of silks and satins. Shakespeare replies to the
question, "Who is Silvia? what is she? that all

our swains commend her?" by telling us that
she is holy, fair and wise, but he does not tell
us that she is exquisitely dressed.  It is almost
impossible to imagine Wordsworth addressing a
serious poem to a well-dressed woman.  Perhaps,
if the dressmakers would get rid of their intolerable jargon, which alarms poets by suggesting
that clothes are a mystery for experts, men of
letters would feel less shy of approaching the
subject.  It is certainly extraordinary that a
theme which moves a far greater number of
human beings to the passionate depths of their
nature than philosophy should be made so little
of in literature.  There is, it seems to me, a great
*Ode to a Dressmaker* to be written, putting into
immortal verse the whirl of emotions that a woman feels in choosing a new frock.  For her the
silkworms, the little silkworms, labour out their
lives.  For her the seal perishes in its ocean cave.
For her the murex is fished up and plants yield
their dyes.  For her the ostrich is tracked down
in the sandy desert and resigns his feathers to
one who can wear them with a better grace.  The
corn falling to the scythe in the field provides
her with the simplest of her hats.  She has borrowed from the fields and the forests, and walks
about clad, not merely in her proper beauty, but
in the general beauty of the earth.  Strange that

she is never content with the result for long. She
turns from the beauty of yesterday as though it
were a faded bouquet, and she moves on towards
the beauty of to-morrow, as restless as Alex-
ander seeking new worlds to conquer. If she has
a fault, it is that she is satisfied to conquer almost any world, if only it is new. There is, so
far as can be seen, no principle in the changes of
her fashions. She does not care whether she has
a high waist or a low waist, or no waist at all;
she cares only for the swift passage from one to
another. She has been compared, in her spring
fashions, to the year in efflorescence. But, after
all, the flowers, if left to themselves, do not
change. It is only when human beings take them
over and cultivate them in gardens that they too
become subject to the fashion of the hour. It is
strange that the ancient poets looked on the
flower of the field as the perfect symbol of im-
permanence. Here, at least, is promise of return.
The flower fadeth, but either in seed or root it is
already preparing to be born again. No such
fate awaits a discarded frock. It may fade into
a shabby second existence, but its glory is brief
almost as a bubble's, and has as complete an end.
Hence those who have spoken of the body as the
garment of the soul have chosen an appropriate
image. There are even religions according to

which the soul, like a woman, changes from one garment to another through æon after æon. It is to be hoped that it does so on some more settled principle—that it is not mere love of change that decides it on dressing up in the body of Julius Cæsar in one century, and in the body of John Smith in another. The soul, it must be admitted, has extraordinary, even freakish, taste in bodies. It regards the human body, perhaps, as fancy dress rather than as a costume for serious use. On any other supposition it would be extremely difficult in some instances to congratulate the soul on its taste. But that leads one into even greater mysteries than the mysteries of dress. And so, having just touched on the relationship between pretty frocks and immortal souls, we may postpone further treatment of the subject till Ascot week returns, bringing other problems and—who can doubt it?—other hats.

# XIII

## THE CRIME OF J. LYONS & CO.

IF Dr. Johnson or Charles Lamb or, indeed, anybody who lived a hundred or two hundred or even three hundred years ago were to return to earth, he would find many changes in the appearance of London. It is doubtful if he would find any other quite so striking as the change that has been brought about by the multiplication of Lyons's tea-shops. There are no other tea-shops that make the same impression on the eye. Their white-and-gold faces and their polished windows are as noticeable as the painted signs of inns. They have a nice suggestion that luxury has been democratised and brought within the reach of anybody who has threepence in his pocket. They announce entertainment. They seem to say that there is no need to go to White Cities in order to be happy while toasted scones may be eaten within from marble tables. Could Sardanapalus himself ask for anything better than to be allowed to sit at a marble table and eat steak-and-

kidney pudding from a silver fork? It is no
wonder that Londoners flock every day in thousands into these white palaces of poached eggs
on toast. They look infinitely more inviting than
the theatres and the picture houses. The Lyons-
going population of London is probably now
greater than the church-going population. There
are Londoners who have never visited the Tower
or been inside Westminister Abbey, but there
are few who have never been in a Lyons's tea-
shop. Even between ten and eleven in the morning you will find some of these shops full. It is
apparently the habit of many people to follow
their cup of bedroom tea and their breakfast
coffee with a cup of coffee on their arrival in the
City as a restorative after the fatigue of the
journey on the Underground. Men, it seems,
must drink something, if only as an alternative
to work. And there is this to be said for coffee
as a drink in the early part of the day, that it
does not fuddle the brain like beer or milk.
Victims of the milk habit, unfortunately, are
also to be seen at Lyons's. You can tell them by
the furtive way in which they creep down side
streets and slip in at the inconspicuous doors
specially provided for them. They have dark
rings under their eyes and never look happy except when actually drinking the "white stuff,"

as they call it among themselves. There is no habit that gets a stronger grip on a man, and the women are, if anything, worse than the men.

I speak from hearsay, but I understand that the first effect produced by a draught of milk is extraordinarily pleasant. Beginners sometimes find the taste nauseating, but the habitual drinker finds even this delightful. The milk, having passed into the stomach, at once sets up a glow through the system and gives the victim a feeling of enormous energy. He feels fit for anything —even for the work that he has been neglecting in order to indulge his craving. He tells himself that, after another glass, he will be able to do it twice as well and twice as fast as he would have done if he had contented himself with drinking a glass of water in the office. His capacity for self-deception increases. He feels amazingly good as well as amazingly buoyant. He achieves wonders in day-dreams. He has, indeed, almost all the characteristics of the alcoholist. He differs from him chiefly through having none of the superficial sociableness and generosity of the spirit-drinker. No milk-drinker ever stands another a glass of milk. The milk-drinker is essentially a solitary—taciturn and forbidding. He prefers to have a table to himself, and, if you did not watch him closely, you might even think that he was unhappy. But, as soon as his lips touch the glass, you can see a look of gratification stealing over his face—a look that he does his best to conceal, lest it should give away his secret. If you attempt to reason with him, he becomes sullen, hostile. He seeks refuge in lying excuses. "Milk is a food," he declares stolidly. "My dear man," you reply to him, "a beer-drinker says the same thing about beer, but, if you read the report of the recent inquiry into alcohol, you will find that beer has no food-value whatever." That exasperates him. "I was not talking about beer. I was talking about milk. I say it's a food. Children live on it." "Yes, the poor little creatures," you reply; "twenty years ago, when children used to be allowed into public-houses, I have seen a mother giving a sip of beer to an infant in arms. She took your view. If you had reproached her, she would have said, 'Beer is a food.' The law has fortunately put a stop to that sort of thing. Why not be frank and admit that you drink milk because you like it?" "I do admit it," he answers, "but I also maintain that it is a food. It is nature's attempt to provide a complete food for calves." "For calves, yes," you take him up, "just as grass is nature's attempt to provide a complete food for cows. Grass and milk are a natural food for the beasts of the field. But man is higher in the scale than a beast of the field and should have nobler tastes." . . . But it is no use trying to convince him. Under the influence of his stimulant, he will say anything. He merely laughs when you remind him that Landru was a milk-drinker and that, on the eve of his execution, when he was offered a half-bottle of wine, he asked for a glass of milk instead. He becomes openly derisive when you remind him that Homer made the odious Polyphemus a milk-drinker in contrast to Ulysses, who drank wine. When the milk has mounted to the brain, men cease to be capable of reasoning.

Lyons's shops must unquestionably be held responsible for a great part of the increase in the habit of milk-drinking during the past twenty years. For some extraordinary reason, the Government, while shutting the public-houses during several hours of the day, permits the sale of milk at all hours. The early morning glass of milk has in consequence become a habit with thousands of people and especially, it is to be feared, with young people. There is no legal age-limit for buying milk as there is for buying alcohol or tobacco. One result of this is that enough money is spent on milk every year to pay for the upkeep of the Army and Navy and

even, it is said, to make England a country fit
for heroes to live in.

It was not, however, in order to discuss or to
deplore the ravages of the milk habit that I sat
down to inveigh against the crime of J. Lyons
& Co. Nothing could have been further from
my thoughts than milk. Deplorable though the
excessive consumption of it is, it would none the
less be ridiculous to describe the sale of it as a
crime. Most of us are far too ready to expend
our moral indignation on things for which we
have no fancy. We are apt to forget that there
are good men and women on both sides of the
question and that, where this is so, it may be
infinitely more harmful to suppress a habit than
to tolerate it, even if it does a considerable
amount of harm. Hence I should be reluctant
to see any but moral pressure brought to bear
on milk-drinkers. They should be dealt with
by the clergy rather than by the police.

The crime of which I accuse Messrs. Lyons is
a much more serious affair than the sale of milk.
It is that they have connived at the destruction
of the charm of London. They have sinned
against good architecture in pulling down a delightful old shop in Coventry Street in order to
make room for an extension of their Corner
House in that region. Before the war this shop,

with its little low windows and its little square panes, attracted the eye every time one passed along the street. It belonged to a jeweller, and its old-fashioned and unostentatious front made one feel that here the tradition of the silversmith must have been handed down from father to son during several generations. This may have been an illusion, but at least the shop was one of the few West End shops that stood like a reminder of the quiet beauty of the town life of a past world. There are not many shops in London that have the air of historical pieces. This was one of them. How the eye brightens at the sight even of the lettering above a shop window or the number on a door that gives one the impression that it has been wrought by an artificer who loved his work! There is something in our nature that craves for design even in the printing of an advertisement. It is not only in painting and in poetry that we long for the presence of the sense of pattern. It is as though we were everywhere in search of delight, and as though the delight of the humblest artificer communicated itself to us in even the least conspicuous pattern it creates. For delight always creates patterns, and patterns in their turn create delight. One of the worst effects of the invention of machinery is that, not only did it make the work in factories mechanical, but it spread the idea of the mechanical even among men who were engaged in the arts and crafts. It would be absurd to deplore the invention of machinery as an absolute evil, but it did produce one notoriously evil effect in lowering the taste for good craftsmanship and in the general subordination of the creative human being to the manufacturing machine. The chief vice of Victorian architecture was that it was for the most part not created but manufactured. There are few shops in London that do not seem to have been turned out with as little creative pleasure as the hardware and earthenware for sale within. London streets, as a consequence, are, so far as the buildings are concerned, among the dullest in the world to walk in. There are signs of a change for the better, but it will be some time yet before it is generally recognised that a shop-front should reveal a personality and enable us to share in the artist's delight in designing it no less than a picture or a poem. If buildings were taken as seriously as pictures or poems, it would not be possible to destroy a charming building without interference. Several countries forbid the export of masterpieces of painting. It is questionable whether it is not even more important to preserve good buildings than good paintings for the mass of the people.

It is melancholy to see a new London that is manufactured taking the place of a London that was built. Nine hundred and ninety-nine buildings in a thousand could easily be spared, but the thousandth, like every work of art, should be regarded as a public possession. Messrs. Lyons have been public benefactors in many respects. Nothing comparable to their genius for catering has ever been known in England before. Genius should recognise genius, however, and the genius that resides in an old shop-front should not be ruthlessly destroyed by the genius of the caterer. The shop in question, indeed, had ceased to be a jeweller's shop before it passed into the hands of Messrs. Lyons. During the war it was taken over by the Air Ministry, who preserved it in its old condition. But now it is gone, and the ghost of a past age has quitted Coventry Street for ever. It will be impossible henceforth to walk down the street without being haunted by the feeling that one is passing the scene of a crime.

# XIV

## THE OLD GAME

As I was passing Westminster Abbey on the top of a bus, a stream of men and women dressed in black was coming out of the porch of St. Margaret's. The bus-conductor paused as he punched my ticket and, jerking his head in the direction of the mourners, nodded and said to me: "A marriage yesterday, a memorial service to-dye, and so the old gyme goes on!" You could not have told whether he was very, very sad or very, very disgusted—whether it was the comedy or the tragedy of human existence that had struck him the more forcibly between punching one ticket and another. He looked too grim for comedy, too cynical for tragedy, but at least he recognised that he was punching small holes in tickets in an extraordinary universe. It gave me a curious pleasure to find so admirable a philosopher on a bus-top. For philosophers are rare. The average man passes through life with scarcely a generalisation to his credit. He makes

a living, and plays games till he is too old for
them, and reads about murders and divorces, but
he is seldom aware of any underlying unity in all
the things he sees, and experiences, and reads
about. It is true that he frequently quotes other
people's generalisations. But these are not his
means of thinking, but his means of avoiding
thought. If he says "East is East and West is
West" it is because this is the easiest way of
dismissing a great problem from his conscious-
ness. He does not wish to disturb his brain or
his soul, and so he goes into hiding behind the
smoke-screen of a platitude. Of two lay preachers who enter the house of the dead, the one who
observes solemnly "In the midst of life we are in
death" is probably he who has been the less profoundly moved by the spectacle of men who
perish like the flowers. Any man who is insensi-
tive enough can produce a platitude for every
occasion. The difference between a platitude
and a generalisation is that in the one case a man
is quoting somebody else's experience and that in
the other he is quoting his own. The objection to
most platitudes is not that they are obvious but
that they are dishonest—that they pretend to be
the expression of far deeper thought and experience than they are. The fact that a thing is
obvious is nothing against it. Nothing could be

more obvious than that man is mortal; but look
what the Psalmist has made of this commonplace.  Look what Shakespeare made of it when
he wrote:

> Golden lads and girls all must,
> As chimney-sweepers, come to dust.

Look what Meredith made of it in "A wind
sways the pines."  Great poetry is for the most
part a reinforcement of the obvious.  It is the
little men who are most afraid of the obvious,
and who would rather tell a falsehood than tell
something that everybody else knows.  As a
matter of fact, among artists it is a great deal
easier to tell a falsehood than to tell an obvious
truth.  For, in order to tell a falsehood, you have
only to contradict a platitude; while, in order to
tell an obvious truth, you have to give life to a
platitude.  "Any fool can tell the truth," said
Samuel Butler, "but it requires a man of some
sense to know how to lie well."  Little literature
is full of such sayings; in great literature they
do not exist.  And, indeed, the saying is merely a
jest the point of which lies in its purpose of
deceiving the unwary.  Butler does not even in
jest attempt to persuade us that it is more difficult to lie well than to tell the truth well, for if
there is one thing that is plain to every artist, it

is that more imagination is required for telling
the truth than for lying. The permanent difficulty of telling the truth for the ordinary writer
is that it is almost impossible to see the truth for
the truisms. The truth has been told so often
before that it has in many instances almost ceased
to be effectively true. It has become familiar
and meaningless, whereas truth, in order to be
really truth, must be as fresh and as full of meaning as though it had never been discovered before
—as bright as a new (pre-war) sixpence.

The bus-conductor, it seemed to me, was
speaking the truth when he made his, in a sense,
commonplace comment on the crowd coming out
from the memorial service. He did not say anything that was not perfectly obvious. But he
said it in a way that convinced one that a perfectly obvious fact had struck a light in his mind.
His "and so the old gyme goes on" was uttered
with a rhythm that suggested that something in
him had vibrated to a universal truth. He had
put two and two together and had been amazed
to find that the answer was four. It was his
amazement, not his answer, that raised the latter
ever so little above a platitude. Most of us re-
serve our amazement for phenomena rather than
for general truths. We are amazed more often
that a batsman should score two hundred than

that a batsman should be mortal. We take the
latter for granted, indeed, and yet it is the more
startling fact of the two. Poetry at least seems
to rise to its greatest heights when the poet remembers the doom of man. It is a fact from
which most of us take refuge in platitudes when
we do not entirely ignore it. Yet literature as
well as religion would lose half its force if it did
not see men against the background of the universal doom. How unaccustomed we are to the
thought of it is shown by the way in which we
are moved, as if by some absolutely new revela-
tion, when a great writer comments on it. Ham-
let has but to take up Yorick's skull and say
to it, "Now get you to my lady's chamber, and
tell her, let her paint an inch thick, to this favour
she must come; make her laugh at that," and we
are thrilled as though we had made a great discovery about human life. The truth is, we are
for the most part indifferent to life as a whole,
and live within a small section of it so absorbedly
that we have no interest in relating this to life in
general. We do not, it may be, live quite in-
coherently. We string our days together on a
thread of money-making or ambition or amusement or love, or mere avoidance of starvation.
But this is the only unity we seek in life, and we
make little effort to see if there is any connection

between our own experience and the experience
of the human race. We are content to be rich
men or lovers or nobodies without looking at ourselves as figures in the eternal procession of rich
men and lovers and nobodies. That is why there
are so few poets and philosophers. The poet and
the philosopher are those who are aware that
there is a procession in things, and who are always looking for the connection between one
thing and another. They may find the wrong
meaning in life, but they are not content till they
have found some meaning, even if it is only that
it means nothing. It is surely a very remarkable instance of the power of generalisation that
such a saying as "Vanity of vanities! All is
vanity" has survived as one of the vital sayings
of the human race for more than two thousand
years. Even a bus-conductor, you would think,
could say something as profound as that, and yet
it required a man of genius to say something
that is as clear as noonday to anyone inclined
to pessimism. In point of fact, however, the
saying becomes obvious only when we believe
it. There is not one life in a million that is
not lived on the assumption that it is not true.
And those of us about whom its truth is most
obvious are the last people of all to recognise it.
We would strenuously deny that those magnifi-

cent appetites of ours for wealth, power or excitement are vanity. We are content to enjoy
them as things in themselves, not as things related to human experience in general or to any
theory of the meaning of the "old gyme."

Philosophic critics have sometimes gone too
far in saying that the greatest poems and the
greatest novels are those which contain the greatest aphorisms. Yet there is something to be said
for the view. The aphorism affords at least one
test by which you can judge a writer. The
Greeks loved to embed gnomic wisdom of this
kind in their literature, and there are few great
writers who have not contributed to the small
stock of the great aphorisms in their language.
Shakespeare, Milton and Wordsworth have
probably bequeathed a greater number of immortal aphorisms than any other English
writers. Pope was also in his way a master of
the aphorism, and, if he was not a great poet, it
was not because he was an aphorist but because
he was the aphorist of other men's thoughts.
Besides, he had a way of leaving in the aphorisms
and leaving out the poetry. But it is almost impossible to think of a poet of the first rank who
did not repeatedly put a general view of life in
a brief phrase. There have been people who have
declared that Keats's "Beauty is Truth, Truth

Beauty" is meaningless, but it was only the identification of truth with beauty that brought
meaning into life for Keats and prevented him
from seeing it as an incoherent waste of phenomena. Every writer has to compose life into the
unity of a picture, and, if he cannot do so, he is
a mere scribbler of things that do not matter.
Not that we can ask a novelist to explain his view
of life in long passages of philosophy. His view
of life as a rule underlies what he writes rather
than interrupts or overruns it. His briefest anec-
dote may be a perfect generalisation about life,
even though it does not contain a single general
statement. It is the artist's method to express
his general view of life in terms of delightfully
particular things. He is a philosopher only in
disguise or when an aphorism flashes out almost
in spite of him. But the novelist, like the philosopher, differs from the rest of us in being able
to see a path of meaning through the wilderness
of phenomena—a path as invisible to most of us
as the track left by a bird in the air. Even the
simplest of us, it is true, hanker after the discovery of some meaning in life, and when a writer
helps to discover one for us in a phrase, we quote
him for a generation. Matthew Arnold said,
"Conduct is three-fourths of life," and it was as
if a new horizon had been disclosed to the Vic-

torians.  It is a phrase that, when we examine
it, looks as if anybody might have said it.  It is
almost inconceivable that the world should have
had to wait thousands of years for this commonplace arithmetical formula about human behaviour.  You would have thought that there
were at least a dozen men in every English village—in every English street, indeed—who
could say something as remarkable.  And yet, if
you were to go from door to door through all the
streets of London, in the hope of finding a man
who could put his view of life in a sentence as
memorable, you would end your mission a con-
firmed pessimist in regard to the philosophic
nature of the human mind.  You would meet
few people who could do more than quote Long-
fellow or Adam Lindsay Gordon or Ella
Wheeler Wilcox as having expressed their larg-
est thoughts.  Plenty of people would be able to
tell you that "life is real, life is earnest," but
scarcely one of them would be able to convince
you that he had thought even this out philo-
sophically for himself.  Man is a parrot, and he
does not even get outside himself and look at
himself as a parrot.  If he did, he would thereby
become a philosopher, and make perhaps a commonplace remark that would be remembered for
centuries.  For most remarks that are worth

making are commonplace remarks.  The thing
that makes them worth saying is that we really
mean them—that they have been mellowed in
our profoundest experiences and are the
"Eureka" of the depths of our nature on discovering that things mean something after all.

## XV

## THE UNEXPECTED

THERE is no use denying it. Life is extraordinarily interesting. Things go on happening, and they are quite often not the things we expected to happen. We can see clearly enough as far as the turn of the road, but beyond that we do not know what surprise may be in store for us. So long as this possibility of surprise remains, there is small chance of our suffering from boredom. We love surprise for its own sake. We like either giving a surprise or getting one. One of the sentences that have lingered in my memory since childhood is a sentence from a nigger minstrel sketch called *The Surprise Party* to which I was taken in a country village, and I fancy I treasure it because it is more crowded with surprise than any other sentence in English literature. It runs: "But the surprise of the party that the surprise party surprised was nothing to the surprise of the surprise party that surprised them." I have forgotten many sentences wiser

and more beautiful than this, but I cannot
grudge a corner of my memory to a sentence so
redundant with the element that keeps life interesting.

Even a Sunday morning at the seaside holds
possibilities of surprise. I went down to spend
the week-end with some friends at a boarding-
house kept by some charming people at Worthing. On Sunday morning I heard a noise of
shooting, but, as I knew there was a war going
on somewhere in the Near East, I did not pay
any particular attention to it. On leaving my
room, however, I found the landlady's daughter
hurrying up the stairs. "Oh, did you hear that
shot?" she cried, breathless with agitation. I
said that I did. "It shot Mrs. ———," she said,
naming the landlady, and trembling in hand and
voice. I can assure you that to hear that your
landlady has just been shot on a quiet Sunday
morning is as surprising a thing as you could wish
to happen to you. You ask: "Where? How?
Who did it? Have you sent for a doctor?" And
you are aquiver with excitement till you hear
that, after all, the landlady is not dangerously
wounded. The shot had come from nowhere,
and had caught her in the back of the neck where
she was washing potatoes beside an open window. It had drawn blood and raised a swelling,

but even by now she had so far recovered that, if
you listened acutely, you could hear the swish of
the water where she was back at work among the
potatoes again. That was the second surprise
—and a happy one. But then the Sunday dinner has to be prepared, no matter who shoots
whom. After a time the villain who fired the
shot was discovered. He was out ratting with
a gun on an allotment on the other side of the
garden wall. One rat, in its effort to escape, had
got up on the top of the wall and was running
along it, when the man fired, missed the rat, and
hit a very estimable lady instead. This, we may
take it, caused a treble surprise. It surprised
the man, it surprised the rat, and it surprised the
lady. Later in the day, when the landlord was
describing the incident, telling how his wife was
standing at the scullery window when the shot
struck her, he added, as though the worst had not
yet been told: "If the window hadn't been open
at the time, it would have been broken." That,
too, was a saying that charmed by its unexpect-
edness. Luckily, in real life, people very seldom
say the inevitable thing. You never know what
people will say. That is what makes their conversation always worth listening to.

If you go to a strange town, however, even to
Worthing, you will come on other unexpected

things besides such, on the whole, melodramatic incidents as the shooting of a landlady. Going out into the country on Saturday afternoon, for instance, I was surprised to find myself standing on a field-path and eagerly taking sides as a spectator in a football match between two teams of which I did not even know the names. One of the teams wore blue-and-white jerseys, the other wore chocolate and black; and, as I am in favor of almost anything blue except Government reports, I felt waves of partisan energy passing from me into the blue-and-white players every time they made a concerted rush towards the other's goal. The centre-forward of the team, I gathered, was called Jerry-Jack—a name somewhat unexpected—and whenever the ball was kicked across within reach of his expert toes there were excited, laughing shouts of "Go on, Jerry-Jack!" in which I silently joined. At last, after rush upon rush, with players tumbling all over the field and jumping quickly to their feet again, Jerry-Jack sent the ball like a bomb past the goal-keeper, and by all the rules I ought to have been more enthusiastic for the blue-and-whites than ever. What was my astonishment, however, to find that I was now filled with an aching desire to see the chocolate-and-blacks scoring a goal and making things equal again.

My sympathies went out especially to one little
chocolate-and-black man with a very red face
and a sweat-soaked mop of very red hair who
always threw the ball in when it was kicked
into touch.  He worked so hard that it was a
sin he should go unrewarded.  I had scarcely
begun to sympathise with him when he leaped
into the air with his head aimed at the ball at
the same time as an enemy player, and fell
back on the field like a dead man.  He was
surrounded and rubbed by players on both sides,
but, in spite of all their rubbing, he seemed un-
conscious when at length they carried him over the
touch-line and laid him on the grass among the
spectators and went on with their game.  A football match, I suppose, is like a Sunday dinner: it
must be gone on with, whatever happens.  But I
confess I felt aggrieved on behalf of the little red
man, as I saw his wounded body lying neglected
and forgotten on the grass while the blue-and-
whites stormed more furiously than ever round
the chocolate-and-black goal.  After a few minutes he was, fortunately, able to sit up, and a minute or two later he was limping back to his place
on the field, and hurrying his dancing mop of
red up and down in search of the hottest forefront
of the battle.  He was chasing after the ball near
the blue-and-white lines when an enemy player

charged into him in a way he obviously thought illegitimate. He left the match to look after itself, and rushed up to the player, with out-stretched arm and finger wagging in fierce ex-postulation, his red face flaming. The referee, seeing the excitement, ran across, seized the player by the right hand, seized the little red man by his, fitted the two right hands together, and, surrounding them with his own, shook them warmly. Smiling and nodding, as much as to say that that was all right, he skipped off again to his work with his whistle. The little red man hesitated. Then he, too, though he did not go so far as to smile, nodded till his mop jumped, and ran off side by side with his enemy towards the thick of the play. O holy spirit of sport, thou that dost lay the evil passions of men and teach them to behave according to the rules even amid the tumult and the shouting of the football field, without thee there could be no civilisation, but only a long contention without law, without honour, without obedience! It is a strange fact that, accustomed though we are to what is called sportsmanlike behaviour, each new instance of it delights us as though it were something that surpassed expectation. It is, no doubt, absurd; but to see such an incident as the little red man shaking hands in reluctant

but unquestioning obedience to the referee increases one's confidence in the future of the
white races.

Even the accidents and incidents of the football field, however, do not bring the surprises of
Worthing to an end. You have only to dip into
a local guide-book to come on plenty of others.
You will find, for instance, that a little way back
from the sea is a village with a church and
cottage associated with Thomas à Becket. Now,
I am not particularly interested in Thomas à
Becket, but it gives me the surprise of the unexpected to discover that he lived near Worthing.
Local associations always produce a thrill in many
of us, even if they are associations with people
who are scarcely more to us than a name in a
school-book. We begin, indeed, almost to like
any famous man who has lived in a town or village
in which we happen to be spending an idle day.
He belongs henceforth to the circle of our associations, if not to the circle of our friends. I shall
always like Tom Paine better because he once
lived in Lewes and because I once read the
medallion saying so in the wall of a house when
I was wandering about the streets with nothing
to do but wait for a train. I shall always like
Sir John Suckling better because he was once
Member of Parliament for Bramber. And now

I suppose I shall always like Thomas à Becket
better because he once lived near Worthing,
where I myself have in all my life spent only
one brief week-end.  And, indeed, if you read
the guide-book, you will discover some surpris-
ingly interesting things about him.  You will
discover that he was connected with the Abbey
of Fécamp in Normandy, and that, probably or
possibly, he was the first man to introduce his
favourite flower, the lily of the valley, from
France into England.  You will also discover,
as further evidence of the ancient connection
between the hinterland of Worthing and the
Abbey of Fécamp, that there is a little Continen-
tal bird that migrates every year to this part of
England alone in order to eat the figs in
Thomas à Becket's garden.  It is called the
beccafico, or fig-eater.  I confess this discovery
gave me almost as great a surprise as the shooting
of the landlady.  It is a delightful notion that
a little foreign bird should cross the sea every
year for hundreds of years and select the figs
in one tiny neighbourhood as though they were
the best of all possible figs.  Were there not figs
at Steyning?  How I should have made any little
foreign bird welcome to the plumpest of them!
Why, this hereditary taste for the Archbishop's
figs is little short of a miracle.  "It can't be

true," I said, as I read it, hoping that it was.
On returning to London, I took down from the
shelves an entirely cold-blooded work, *The Hand-
Book of British Birds,* and turned up "Fig-
Eater" in the index.   The index, alas! referred
me to "Garden Warbler," and under "Garden
Warbler" I read:

"This is the *pettychaps, beccafico,* or *fig-eater*
of Willughby and Ray (*Orn.,* pp. 216, 217).
Jesse was assured by a resident at Worthing,
'that the *beccafico* annually visits the fig orchard
near that place,' and he supposed (erroneously)
that it was found in no other part of England
('Gleanings,' iii., p. 78)."

That, I am afraid, is law-court evidence, and,
when a man is able to quote things in brackets,
the finest story in the world vanishes—for me,
at least—into thin air.   Luckily, the birds of
real life are so differently distributed in different
places that their appearance always produces as
delightful a surprise as any story of the birds of
the imagination.   And so a London dweller,
walking along by the sea at Worthing, will be
charmed by the wheatear in the white skirt, that
flies away in a semicircle over the rust-coloured
shingle and hides in the tamarisk, its tail jerking
nervously.   The little ringed plovers, too, come
when the tide is out and run over the wet sand

with the speed of insects. As they fly off in a
cloud with a silver lining at one's approach, they
utter that mournful, appealing whistle that is
like a cry of small, frightened bird-ghosts, and
that makes even the sands of a watering-place
seem desolate as the shores of an uninhabited
island. And then there are the sandpipers,
marching from side to side, with their long, pry-
ing bills and devouring the helpless inhabitants
of the sands that sometimes dance around their
feet and set the sandpipers dancing round after
them. They are unexpectedly tame little birds
that do not run away from a human being more
than is necessary. Indeed, they are too busy
looking for things to eat to notice a human
being. Thus life, as we have agreed, is full of
surprises. And I shall have another surprise if
some ornithologist does not tell me that the bird
I saw was not a sandpiper at all, but a dunlin.
If he does, I shall be surprised that a dunlin's
bill should be so much. longer than it is in the
pictures in the bird books. It is clear, in any
case, that the unexpected may happen at Worthing as anywhere else. It is a good argument in
favour of going away for the week-end.

# XVI

## THE STUDENT

It is in the autumn that one used to puff oneself out with good resolutions about learning. One prepared to receive professors. With what pleasure one bought new books! One felt as if one were setting out on a journey. It is one of the great pleasures of a student's life to buy a heap of books at the beginning of the autumn. Here, he fancies, are all the secrets. An annotated Euripides, a text-book on natural philosophy, a book of logarithms, Morris's *Philology*, Maine's *Ancient Law*, the first book of *The Faëry Queene*, *Rasselas* with notes, Professor Gilbert Murray's *Greek Literature*, Mommsen, Cruttwell, the *Histories* of Tacitus in a red binding— he opens each of them impartially with pleasure; he enjoys the very "feel" of the paper, the smoothness or roughness of the covers, the look of the title-page. He could hardly relish them more if they were things with a sweet smell or taste. That at least is the experience of one who always loved his books to be new and shrank from getting them second-hand as one would shrink from a sweetmeat that had first been in somebody else's mouth. The fresh, white pages that no thumb had sullied attracted me possibly as a symbol of a new beginning, a dawn, a spring. Now I could rise from my past as from sleep, put on "the new man," as the preachers say, and set out on a career of tireless discovery. I would plunge into the beautiful waters of learning and emerge a scholar. I would study even sound in the physics room, for sound was in some way related to Schubert, and to master all that dull pose about vibrations and the length of organ-pipes might be an initiation into the deeper mysteries of music. The truth is, every subject was a hill to climb, and any hill was better than no hill. I felt a certain excitement as I read *The University Calendar* and came on the courses even in strange subjects such as engineering and political economy. I could fancy myself with the greatest of ease a civil engineer and an architect, even though algebraic formulæ meant less to me than the marks left by the feet of seagulls on the sand, and though I could hardly draw a house correctly enough to distinguish it from a beehive. The sense of my ignorance and incapacity did not daunt me in those days. I regarded these as remediable weaknesses. I accepted the world

as a great lucky-tub into which, did I but dip
earnestly enough, I could find whatever talent I
desired. How often did I seriously consider the
possibility of becoming a sculptor or a composer!
I felt that if I began to handle the clay with
all my might it would take shape from some
of those restless dreams and cravings that made
it so delightful to be idle to-day and promised to
come to birth in something real and beautiful
to-morrow. As for turning composer, my in-
ability to play any musical instrument did not
chill my hopes on an evening on which I had
heard *Adelaïde* or the "Prize Song" in the
*Meistersingers* sung. Here was a world into
which to break through—why not break through
into it? I read somewhere that Schumann did not
learn to play the piano till he was in his twenties.
He even had some sort of operation on his fingers, did he not? in order to rid them of the stiff-
ness of maturity. Could I not do the same?
Alas, three consecutive evenings of five-finger
exercises cured me of my dream of becoming a
second Schumann. Not beauty, but tedium, lay
that way. For knowledge of music, I had to
content myself with Grove's Dictionary.

There are some students who, fortunately or
unfortunately for themselves, have none of these
illicit longings for impossible careers. They have

not a single feather in their heads. They seem to decide what they are going to be on the day on which they leave school, and to take nothing seriously that does not lead them straight to the Church, the Bar or the Civil Service. There are others who for the moment do not decide upon any career save the career of examinations. They take upon themselves the routine of the year's work and would regard any mental effort made outside the beaten track as wasted energy. They would regard it as frivolous to read Gibbon if Dr. William Smith falls in more aptly with their course of studies. Literature is to them a subject, not a delight. They regard Aristophanes not as amusing, but as a collection of answers to examination questions. Æschylus is not a poet, but a huge pudding of variant readings. Everything is of value, not in so far as it answers questions put by one's own nature, but in so far as it can answer questions likely to be put by an examiner's ingenuity. This type of student is, I believe, disappearing; the modern theory of education discourages him. It is not very long, however, since he was the ideal of the professors and schoolmasters. They loved him because his virtues were so measurable. He was told to collect a certain number of facts, and the success with which he did his work could be appraised

at a glance.  At the same time, we must not
think that the professors and schoolmasters were
only consulting their ease in idealising this kind
of student.  His success did involve certain necessary virtues—obedience, thoroughness, self-disci-
pline, the cultivation of the organising faculty.
On the other hand, it implied such an economy of
curiosity and imagination that these were frequently atrophied from disuse.  He was more
likely to achieve a successful career than a successful life.  I knew a student of this kind who
never read a single book—either as a schoolboy
or as undergraduate—that did not bear directly
on an examination.  He shunned Pater as he did
*Tit-Bits.*  Wordsworth, like *Comic Cuts,* was,
for him, reading for idlers.  He had a brilliant
career, and ended in a high position in the Civil
Service, and I cannot deny that he always
seemed perfectly happy.  But it is a question
worth debating whether, if he had been less suc-
cessfully educated, he might not have been a
better educated man.  He had a good mechanism
for learning—rather than a mind.  Were all men
educated on the same pattern as he, we should
have a fine race of officials so far as the routine
of officialism is concerned, but no inventors, no
statesmen of imagination, no poets, no leaders.
It was probably of the over-disciplined, over-

routined student that Professor Laurie was thinking when he pleaded with the richer sort of parents to throw their children sufficiently on their own resourses, to give them "some of the advantages of the gutter." Many people, on the other hand, are nowadays almost too devotedly in love with the gutter as the school of originality. They imagine you have only to set an infant or a young man carefully in the gutter in order to release a wealth of fine impulses that will save him both in this world and the next. The truth is, education should be neither all formalism and routine, nor all an affair of desultory impulses. Here, as elsewhere, discipline and indiscipline must balance one another, and the result will be better than a monopoly of either. Reading Professor John Adams's admirable book, *The Student's Guide,* I cannot help thinking with envy of the student who can subject himself to system even to the point of beginning his work with the subject he likes least and of knowing to within five minutes how long he will spend each evening on each subject. The picture of the ideal student rises in my mind as I read: I see him trampling on irrelevant day-dreams, and submitting himself to obedience through the impulse towards mastery. I remember how for myself, I studied as an Epicurean. But I always

regarded the ideal student as an ascetic, and I
never luxuriated more blissfully in Epicureanism
than when I was dreaming I was an ascetic
myself.

Thus, as a student, one had two dreams. One
had the dreams of getting knowledge, and one
had the dreams of getting character. The night-
watches were pleasant with the thought of making oneself a master of both. One went to sleep
in a cloud of ambition. But in the morning Epicurus prevailed again. There would be someone
in the porch of the college who would meet me in
an idle mood and insist on a walk along the tow-
path of a canal or who had been reading a book
and wanted to argue that no one existed except
himself, or who believed that Thoreau was a better writer than Emerson, or that *The Shop Girl*
was a better musical comedy than *The Geisha.*
There was always some good reason for ignoring
Latin and for passing by logic on the other side.
Those were still the days of the æsthetic period,
and one could, with a good conscience, prefer the
shadows of the willow-trees in the olive-green
waters of the canal to the dreary humour of Plautus—at least, of Plautus studied, like a corpse,
in small sections, and with an eye to his gram-
mar rather than to his jokes. . . . One certainly
would not for anything have missed one's stu-

dent days. To mix with other students is an education in itself. It is to come into touch with ideas that are "living creatures having hands and feet." One may leave their society, ignorant of "why peninsulas more frequently turn southward than northward, why the jute industry settled down in Dundee"; but one becomes in their company a citizen of a larger world, a sharer in the world's interests, one who is liberated at least into the atmosphere of great traditions. Thus does every man attempt to find arguments in favour of the education he himself has had. The man who has had a University education believes it is the only education worth having. The man who is self-educated believes in self-education as the secret of success. The man who idled at college explains what a blessing his idleness has been to him. The man who has read his eyes out praises God for his labours. Thus, when we look back, we all turn out to have been model students. . . . At the same time, if one had it all to do over again, how eagerly one would consult the pages of Professor Adams for good advice! How one would plunge into an enthusiasm for work! And —how one would find oneself the next morning far from the droning lecture-room, smoking a pipe of Navy Cut and discussing the immortality of the soul under the blackening elms of the park!

# XVII

## A DEFENCE OF SUPERSTITION

IT was announced shortly before the production of *The Golden Moth* that the name of the play was to be changed because the company believe that the presence of the word "golden" in a title is unlucky. A little later the management of the theatre decided to defy superstition and the play was produced with the original title after all. The stage is perhaps the most superstitious institution in England, after the racecourse. The latter is so superstitious that to wish a man luck when on his way to a racemeeting is considered unlucky. Instead of saying "Good luck!" you should say something insulting, such as, "May you break your leg!" Actors and actresses have not only all the ordinary superstitions about the picking up of pins, breaking looking-glasses, and the unluckiness of certain numbers. They have also a number of professional superstitions. It is unlucky, they say, for instance, to quote *Macbeth*. Actors dare not say to each other at parting: "When shall we three meet again?" No good actress would advise a nervous fellow-artist to "screw her courage to the sticking-place." It is unlucky during rehearsals to quote the catchword of a forthcoming play in casual conversation. It is unlucky to carry a make-up box, like an amateur actress. Then there are certain theatres that are regarded as unlucky, and the superstitious actor is depressed at the prospect of having to appear at one of them. The luck may turn, we are told, if the name of the theatre is changed; this was probably the cause of the change of the name of one London theatre which has since been successful.

Most of us are accustomed to regard superstitious people as unenlightened, and there is no one who feels more eminently wise than the man who rises first from a table at which thirteen guests have sat down. So far as I have discovered, however, the dividing line between those who are superstitious and those who are not is not at all the same as the line that divides enlightenment from unenlightenment. Some of the world's wisest men have been superstitious. Some of the world's greatest dunderheads have been free from superstition. Plutarch was a wise man, not only for his own age, but for any age, yet he believed in superstitions that a modern bus-conductor would laugh at. Many of those who laugh at superstitions do so from narrowness of mind. They are incredulous of everything that their eyes have not seen. They cannot imagine anything outside the day's work and the football results. Their unbelief in black cats is simply a form of dull materialism. I do not, I may say, contend that the superstitious man is wiser than the unsuperstitious. All I contend is that freedom from superstition is not necessarily a form of wisdom, but that it frequently results from thoughtlessness. Perfect wisdom, I believe, gives perfect freedom from superstition, but it probably involves belief in a good many things that will seem superstitious to a thoughtless man.

Consider, for a moment, how the first superstition came into the world. Man found himself cast into a chaos of drifting phenomena without the slightest notion of what they meant or whether they meant anything. He could not distinguish between things and their shadows. He was as ignorant as a child as to how children were born. He did not know what was happening to his friends when they died. He was frightened of many things, because some things hurt him, and he did not know which did and which did not. All that he knew was that queer things were constantly happening, but they happened, not according to any rule that he could see, but in a confused and terrifying jumble. One day, in the forest, however, he casually picked up a pin —or, let us say, a sharp pine-needle—and immediately afterwards he came on the most delightful bunch of bananas he had ever tasted. This did not at the moment strike him as being remarkable. But the next day he noticed the same sort of pine-needle lying on the ground and picked it up. Immediately afterwards he discovered another bunch of bananas even more delightful than the first. His brain swam with the sense of discovery. He beat his forehead with his hands—hairy, prehensile hands—for the birth of something absolutely new in his mind was making his head ache. He muttered: "I pick up pine-needles and find sweet bananas! I pick up pine-needles and find sweet bananas!" It was some time before even this conveyed a clear message to a brain unaccustomed to act. But as he repeated the words in a sort of trance, the truth suddenly flashed on him. When he uncovered his face, he was looking ten years older, but he was wearing a smile that was almost human. He did not exactly say to himself, "I have found a pattern in the universe," but he had made the first move towards the happiest of all Eurekas. He was never quite simian again.

He was like a child who, after long contempla-
tion of the stars in the night sky, that seem to lie
about haphazard like fallen apples, suddenly
picks out the certain pattern of a constellation.
He, too, has seen a pattern: the stars are no
longer an abracadabra to him, but reveal meaning after meaning to him in a speech that he
continually learns to understand better. In the
same way, primitive man in his superstitions was
slowly learning to put two and two together.
What matter if they often came to five? It is
better to put two and two together wrong than
to believe that they cannot be put together at all.

This, it may be said, may account for the
reign of superstition, but it does not therefore
justify the superstitions of civilized men and
women. We have surer means nowadays of
discovering the pattern in life. We cannot be
content with apparent cause and effect, but we
employ intelligent tests for the discovery of the
real cause. The child in arms may believe that
the watch flies open because it blows hard on its
back, but a grown-up man would be an imbecile
to imagine that this is the real reason why the
watch flies open. This is true enough. When
the real pattern of cause and effect is known,
there is no room for fantastic explanations.
We have not the right to believe that the crowing

of cocks causes the sun to rise, or that railway
trains are propelled, not by steam, but by the
waving of a green flag, or a green light. One
might as well doubt the pattern of the Seven
Stars. Such patterns are established once for
all. On the other hand, the greater part of the
universe is undiscovered and uncharted, as the
greater part of the sky is. Our lives are still a
voyage amid chance and confusion, and there are
many things of which we know as little as the
first monkey. While this continues, men will
go on being superstitious—casting their fancies
into the unknown in search of signs. For superstition is mainly a belief in signs. The superstitious man does not believe that bringing
blackthorn in flower into a house actually causes
a death in the house; what he believes is that
it announces a death. It is the same with
telling fortunes with the cards. The cards
are not supposed to control events but only to
prophesy them. I know that the superstitious
do not always adopt this comparatively philo-
sophical attitude. Some of them will put the
blame of their misfortunes on a friend, for
instance, who has sent them a gift of white
flowers without a mixture of other colours. But
this is unreasonable. The only reasonable defence of modern superstition I have ever heard

was that certain signs show the direction of events as a weathercock shows the direction in which the wind is blowing.

Even so, in practice, it is at times almost impossible to distinguish between the prophet of bad news and the causer of bad events. In the old days the prophets were stoned because they were hated as a woman hates a broken mirror. I have heard superstitious people arguing gravely as to whether President Wilson's downfall was caused by his association with the number thirteen, or whether his association with the number thirteen was a prophecy of his downfall. It will be remembered that on his arrival in France he was entertained at a dinner at which thirteen persons sat down, because he had announced that he regarded thirteen as a lucky number. It will also be remembered that, though he originally published his Fourteen points, they were afterwards reduced to thirteen, owing to the objections of the Allies to the "Freedom of the Seas." The superstitious find it difficult to think that this was only an omen. They half believe at the back of their minds that another guest and another point might have made the world safe for democracy.

The ordinary man's reply to superstitions of the kind is seldom based on reason. He is content to say "Rot!" and will no more argue about it than if you told him that a runner duck in your back-yard had been heard quoting *Paradise Lost*. As a matter of fact, neither the attack on superstition nor the defence of it has very much to do with reason. We believe or disbelieve according to our temperaments. Two men, equal in brain and courage, will behave quite differently when it comes to walking under a ladder or lighting a cigarette from a match from which two cigarettes have been already lit. Parnell was eminent for moral courage, but he believed that green was an unlucky colour, and was horror-stricken—and not on æsthetic grounds —when he was presented with a green smoking-cap by a too patriotic lady. During the war the men who carried mascots were not noticeably inferior to the men who did not. By a curious irony, it was in the country which instituted the worship of reason that mascots were most popular. An interesting essay could be written on the theme that an increase of rationalism leads automatically to an increase of superstition. I doubt whether the religious Victorians, who sneered at ghosts and picked up pins only on grounds of economy, were quite so superstitious as their irreligious successors. After all, the human mind cannot be content to accept the unknown as un-

knowable.  Life is a mystery, but most of us feel
that, like a jigsaw puzzle, it may yield a solution
if only we keep trying to put the apparently incoherent pieces together.  Superstition will never
give us the whole pattern, but it is a pardonable
attempt to unite two or three of the pieces in a
sub-pattern.  All science and art is but the piec-
ing together of a sub-pattern out of chaos.  Be
not censorious if an inhabitant of chaos finds a
meaning you do not in two magpies or a dog's
howl or a slice of bread-and-butter that falls with
its face in the dust.

# XVIII

## THE CHOCOLATE BUS

I CANNOT help regretting the appearance of the chocolate bus in the streets of London. Not that I object to a bus of a new colour. On the contrary, I have long held that the motor bus is an unworthy successor to the old horse bus, chiefly because the horse buses used to pour down Piccadilly in as many colours as you will find in a box of paints, while the motor buses scuttle along after one another in a wearisome monotony of red, as empty of personality as strings of mechanical lobsters (boiled ones). But, if it was necessary to introduce a new colour on to the streets, the last of all the colours I would wish to see there is chocolate-brown. The one drawback to chocolate is its colour. Charming to the taste, it is dull to the eye. One would never eat it if one did not know from experience that it tastes better than it looks. It is, no doubt, in accordance with the great principle of compensation that runs through life that the birds

of least brilliant colour sing the most brilliant
songs, and that the sweetmeats of poorest favour
should have the richest flavour. But a bus is
neither a bird nor a sweet meat, and should be
painted red, yellow, orange, blue, green, indigo
or violet.

Even so, it was not chiefly on account of its
colour that I had a sense of grievance when I saw
a chocolate bus the other day stealing for the
first time along a route that takes me within a
hundred yards of my door. I should have objected equally to a bus of any other colour in the
circumstances. I have for some time past been
doing my best not to ride in buses, and I have
often succeeded by the simple process of being ex-
cluded from their overcrowded and malodorous
maws. I have said, with the other patient inhabitants of at least one suburb of London, "This is
disgraceful," and have vowed a lifelong abstin-
ence from bus-riding. But no sooner do I see
a bus drawing up with a seat empty—or with a
piece of floor-space empty—than my hand
reaches out for it as a dipsomaniac's for a for-
bidden bottle, and, the next minute, I find myself
as ever imprisoned in the Black Hole of the
vehicle, rocking through the streets in an unnatural attitude, with vibrations beyond endur-
ance entering my heels and jigging their way

upwards through every bone till they reach my
skull, which is only protected by my hat from
the roof that bangs it sideways at every jolt.
"This," I say to myself, as the bag I am carrying in my free hand lurches into the paper an
ill-natured old gentleman is trying to read, "is
life. This," I meditate, "is the civilisation we
Europeans are trying to spread over the world.
This is the fulfilment of the dreams of the Greeks
and the Romans and all the great civilising races.
To be bumped about in a bus—how unfortunate
is the South Sea Islander, lolling lazily by his
lagoon, to have missed so uplifting an experience! How melancholy is the lot of the Fijian,
who walks from place to place, like a beast, instead of riding in the belly of a mechanical
rhinoceros, like a man!" Thus I reflect, not without bitterness, as I actually pay money to the
conductor for being allowed to squeeze myself
into a place in which if a murderer or a bigamist
were confined he would justly complain that
prison life was being made intolerable. If gaol
were anything like the inside of a motor bus with
"standing-room for five only," no man, who was
not either mad or a born criminal, would risk
committing any offence likely to send him there.
I can think of no more effective kind of prison
reform than to abolish the prisons and commit

criminals to insides of motor buses instead. Imagine what a sentence of "a month" would be in those circumstances. Hour after hour, day after day, to hang on to a rail and bump and sway and stagger and vibrate through one street that is duller than another, and another that is even duller than that—to be able to read nothing but advertisements of soaps and gas mantles and boot polish—never to feel the wind of heaven except in the form of a draught that is half dust and half other people's breathing—to be crowded with other human beings into a space into which one could not endure being crowded even with one's most admired friends—Dante might have included such a punishment among the torments of the *Inferno*. There is no advantage in it that I can think of, except that it takes you faster than you would otherwise go to some place or other that is not worth going to. That is why I would limit the use of the insides of motor buses to convicts. Did not the ancients punish criminals in a similar way by putting them in barrels filled with spikes and rolling them down a hill?

Having reached this point in my quarrel with motor buses, I may seem illogical in greeting so testily a new line of buses that should help to relieve the congestion. If I do so, however, I have a good enough reason. At the moment when the first chocolate bus appeared on my home route, I had just become so impatient of all motor buses that I had determined to learn to walk again—an art that I had almost forgotten. One day I actually did walk. I found it an exceedingly pleasant form of movement. There was a sort of natural rhythm in it. I no longer felt that I was being thrown about by some force infinitely more powerful than myself from one London borough to another. I could pad along as gently as an old dog. I could amble at my ease like a hen picking up her dinner. I could stop whenever I liked at a shop-window and look at a case of eighteenth-century spoons, or at an array of Dundee cakes, or at a travelling-trunk that I would like to buy if I had the money to travel, or at the picture on the wrapper of Miss Ethel Dell's new novel, or at a necklace of pearls that I would sell if somebody gave it to me, or at the price-tickets on the plums and the celery at a greengrocer's. Even this, however, is only a small part of the pleasure of walking when one might be riding on a motor bus. The greatest pleasure of all is to realise that there is no hurry, and to escape from this universal folly of rushing at full speed to a place that is no better than the place one is at already. It is a law of nature that we must keep moving. The sheep in the

field does it, the fly on the window-pane, the
sparrow on the road. Everywhere living things
are doomed to hop or dance or saunter in order
that they may keep alive. But the movement
that is necessary to live is not movement from
one place to another; it is merely rhythmical
exercise of wing or limb, with no vulgar object
of arriving anywhere in particular. The gnats
that swing up and down in an elastic cloud are
not bent upon going anywhere. I doubt if they
are even looking for something to eat. It is
merely that they know by instinct that it is more
pleasant to keep eternally moving like the
planets than to sit still like a heap of stones. Man
is the only one of the animals that has attempted
to escape from this perpetual round of motion,
and to stiffen into stillness while he is yet neither
a cripple nor dead. He desires to go somewhere
else than where he is, but he does not desire to
move. Hence, in his cunning, he has invented
means after means of being moved. He has
abandoned activity for passivity till he has almost achieved his ideal of being hurried to some
unimportant destination like one of a heap of
paving-stones rattled along in a truck in the
wake of a traction-engine.

He reached this extreme of passivity only by
slow stages. He began by mastering the more

pliable animals and compelling them to carry
him. While he rode on horseback, however, he
may be said to have exchanged one kind of
motion for another. The rider is still active in
his movements; his muscles tighten and loosen
in as musical a rhythm as the rhythm of walking.
He has become a centaur instead of a man.
Similarly, in the invention of the rowing-boat,
man simply increased the range of his rhythms.
He came nearer his ideal of being moved instead
of moving with the invention of wheels and sails.
He rejoiced as he freed his muscles from the
delights of effort, but even then he experienced
exquisite and subtle pleasures of movement in
slackening and tightening reins, and in the skil-
ful use of helm and sail. His temptation to idleness increased as vehicles and ships grew in size.
He no longer wished to drive or to manage the
boat. He was content to be driven by a horse
that he himself did not know how to drive, and
to use a ship as a travelling bed-sitting-room.
This indolence of his gave men of mechanical
minds their chance. Seeing what a lazy creature
was man, they invented railways and ocean liners
and chars-à-bancs and motor buses and underground tubes in which they could transport the
poor creature in bulk endlessly from place to
place, without the slightest effort on his part,

except that of putting his hand in his pocket
and bringing out money to pay for his ticket.
So that at the present day the human race is
becoming in ever a greater and greater degree
a race of passengers. Could anything look less
like a happy flock of jackdaws or an ecstatic
dance of gnats than the mob of human beings
that we see jumbled together to-day in an underground train? They are shaken as you might
jingle the money in your pocket, but they do not
move. They are in a hurry, but the beauty of
swiftness does not course through their beings.
Set on the loveliest of the planets, with streams
flowing, with a pearly moon rolling across the
daylight sky, with birds singing in the trees, with
children romping under them, they neglect all
this noble spectacle amid which they were meant
to loll or to labour in order to shut themselves
inside a lighted box on wheels, and to be borne
at top speed through the dull viewlessness of
the underworld. And the motor bus, though
it remains above ground, is a box on wheels that
hurries the inside passenger through a world almost as unrefreshing to the eye. One has no
more life, as one sits in it, than a posted letter.
One's destination has become everything; one's
journey to one's destination nothing—nothing,
at any rate, but a necessary evil. This is against

all wisdom, which bids us enjoy the journey no less than the end of the journey—which bids us keep moving, even if we are moving nowhere in particular.

If the human race, in abandoning the pleasures of physical movement, were finding compensation in new pleasures of the movement of mind or spirit, there would be more to be said in behalf of motor buses. But look at the map of the world, and you will search in vain for even a village in which there is evidence of any movement of mind or spirit such as filled all Italy with beauty four hundred years before the first motor bus had rattled human flesh and bones through the streets of London. Things being what they are, I wish the new chocolate bus every success. I shall most certainly use it. But I shall use it regretfully, thinking of all those fine walks I have been robbed of under plane-trees and the spiky green balls of their fruit—past booksellers' and jewellers' and fruiterers' and tobacconists' shops and pawnbrokers' with their honourable and ancient sign.

# XIX

## RIDING ON A CHAR-À-BANC

THE country, they say, is being ruined. Some people blame the Government; others lay the chief blame on the char-à-banc. There is no English institution more intensely hated than the char-à-banc. Everybody who is not sitting in it loathes the very sight of it. It is, in their view, a means by which English cities empty their most objectionable inhabitants into the country on Sundays. It is a monster with a taste for beauty-spots, and the more delightful is the Eden you have chosen out of all the world to live in, the more certain is it to be invaded by this mechanical wild beast, with its horn roaring like a wounded alligator and its forefeet pounding the dust into the air till it chokes the very birds in the middle of their songs and leaves a mantle of filth on every flower. If the people sitting in the char-à-banc were enjoying themselves we might forgive this outrage on the Sabbath peace. But a mere glance tells us that they are incapable of enjoying themselves. For one thing, they are packed so tight that their sole emotion must be a deep and growing mutual hatred. Then they can see nothing, because they are enveloped in the moving cloud of dust raised by the other char-à-banc just ahead. They also live in constant fear of losing their lives, for the chauffeurs of chars-à-bancs are, as a rule, men who drove tanks in France and who regard all manner of obstacles as things best taken with a rush. These men will tear down a steep hill, with a sudden curve at the end of it leading to a giddy bridge with a low parapet, as though the chief aim of their lives were hairbreadth escapes. Like the Lord Chancellor, they would rather be feared than despised as they dash through the villages and country lanes, scattering cyclists and hens to both sides of the road. Last year the passengers tried in these circumstances to keep up their courage by singing. But the police authorities objected, and even this dismal substitute for happiness is no longer permitted. Occasionally the char-à-banc stops in a village—always at a public-house—and the occupants get out and make a pretence of dancing. When they have had a quarter of an hour's beer they often form in a ring in the middle of the road and sing *Auld Lang Syne*. They are, many of them, queer-

looking people with fat in the wrong places.
They are mostly red, and they laugh at
nothing, as when they make such remarks as,
"Just needed that drop of beer, Geordie!" or
"'Oo said the ashes were lost? I've got 'em in
my eye." Worse than this, they behave as
if the village belonged to them and not to the
inhabitants. They twit the local sergeant. They
would twit the rector if he came along. They
have lost all that self-consciousness—that dread
of appearing foolish to other people—which is
so charming an element in the behaviour of
Englishmen. They are sober, but they behave
as if they were tipsy. Meanwhile they have
turned our village from a rural retreat into
an imitation of the Mile End Road on Jubilee
night. Yes, there is a great deal to be said
against them. I have said only a small part of it.

Circumstances change most. things, however,
and, if you go for a ride in a char-à-banc, you do
not see yourself as a red, rude person—a de-
stroyer of the haunts of ancient peace. I found
myself in a strange city on Sunday afternoon,
and, if ever you have been in a strange English
city on Sunday, you will know how it seems as
though you realised for the first time that the
world is the dullest possible planet that anybody
could have made. Every house seems to be dead.

Even the summer sun is able to reveal nothing
but a monotony of death. The passers-by are
going nowhere in particular. They have neither
work nor play, but are just putting in time.
They are neither asleep nor awake. They
have as little apparent vitality as empty
salmon tins scattered on a piece of waste land.
Coming on such a scene of desolation, a long
yellow char-à-banc seems a thing of beauty and
an emissary of hope. It carries in front a board
with the name of somewhere in the country
printed on it, and the offer to take you there and
back for five shillings. You rejoice at the possibility of escaping so cheaply. You do not think
of the feelings of the people who have bought
houses in the place you are going to invade. You
are not aware of harbouring any evil intentions
against them. You are thinking only of the
beauty of spread-out fields and the swift passage
of scene after scene and the chance of seeing a
hill or a wood or a river. You get into the char-à-
banc, which seems the most innocent of wild
beasts. You look round at the other passengers,
and you see that they bear no resemblance whatever to the rubicund male and female villains
whom you had always seen on chars-à-banc from
the road. An old man with a yellow face, a yellow dewlap and grey hair at the base of his bowl-

er hat sits and smokes a huge pipe meditatively
by the side of his little granddaughter, whom he
is taking out for a day's jaunt.  A middle-aged
father of a family has brought his wife and small
son, for whom he tries to get a seat beside the
driver.  There are several pairs of lovers—some
of the kind that will marry, some of the kind that
won't.  Two women have come together; two
youths have come together.  There are also men
who, like yourself, have come alone and are content to sit and smoke and say nothing.  You could
not have a quieter crowd; you could not have a
quieter chauffeur.  He certainly does raise a dust
and make a noise, but you leave the dust behind
you, and the noise is at least better than running
into people round the corner.  He does not even
stop at the public houses.  He passes "The
Chained Bull" at twenty miles an hour.  There
is a good deal of bumping as he tears over the
ground, but it is not much worse than being
knocked about by a boxer.  As you approach the
beauty-spot you find other chars-à-bancs con-
verging on it from all quarters.  The dust is certainly becoming a little thick, but if you cough,
you don't swallow very much of it.  Then your
char-à-banc takes its place in the procession.
You grind and grunt slowly over a bridge and up
a corkscrew hill, and work your way into the

market square of the town, where you find that
all the other chars-à-bancs in England have got
there before you.  There are rows and rows of
them packed as tightly as herring-boats in a har-
bour.  The tea-shops in the square are all
crowded, and, if you are wise, you stroll away in
the hope of finding some idler spot.  You make
your way past a ruined castle and walk down a
path that takes you to the bottom of a steep cliff,
and a rather well-dressed little boy begins to run
by your side and talk to you in a whining voice.
You think he is trying to tell you that his father
is ill, or that one of his companions has had an
accident, till suddenly you catch something about
"the last battle of the Civil War," and you realise that he is telling you the history of the place
for gain.  You probably did not know it had a
history; but it knows.  It announces it on boards
—every place where a wall has fallen in—and
offers to let you see dungeons and such pleasant
sights for sixpence.  You wander on in search of
a tea-shop, and another little whining boy trots
alongside you and laments over the "last battle
of the Civil War."  You see people approaching
in the opposite direction, and beside each of them
is a little running boy pouring out his sing-song
about this extremely lugubrious but lucrative
battle.  In the end you buy a guide-book to find

out what it is that all the little boys have been
trying to tell you.  You discover that you have
arrived in one of the most famous places in England, though you did not know about it twenty-
four hours ago.  You learn that there are enough
wonderful things to see to keep you busy for a
week.  After tea you go off to see the petrifying
well and the hermit's cave and the wishing well,
into which woman after woman thrusts her arm
while her friends remind her, "You mustn't tell
what you wish."  You are quite exhausted by the
time you have gone the round of these things and
begin to feel as learned as the keeper of Egyptian antiquities in the British Museum.

The public-houses open just before you start
home, and barmen are kept busy supplying beer
for the gentlemen and stout for the ladies.
After a humane interval, we are all collected,
and the return journey begins.  The road is now
packed with chars-à-bancs. Dust flies in simoons,
and the chars-à-bancs fly too.  By this time we
are beginning to feel arrogant and to resent the
presence of any other traffic on the road.  One
char-à-banc knocks down a girl cyclist, and the
procession is brought to a halt, while all the
chars-à-bancs behind blow their horns and impatient passengers call out "Hurry up!"  "Oh,
get on!"  "What does a bicycle matter?"  The

girl is luckily not dead, but the incident has jarred our nerves, and we draw up at the next public-house to discuss the matter. The evening air is cold, and, as the char-à-banc seems inclined to stay there for ever, the passengers dismount one by one and go inside. The old yellow man comes out again, waits awhile in the cold, and then reflects that there is just time for another one and goes back. He comes out again, takes his seat, feels cold, realises that there is probably time for a final one, and again goes back. After a while we get started, but at the end of another few miles another public-house requires us to pull up. . . . There is a little man inside singing—or, rather, groaning—about "that little cottage in the winding lane." When we get going again the stout has made the ladies laugh easily. The lovers have boldly put their arms round each other, and the father of the family looks round on them all knowingly and benignly. We do not sing, but we could do so on slight provocation. When we almost run down a cyclist we jeer, and the father of the family leans over the side of the char-à-banc and shouts at him scornfully, "Get out of it!" as we fly past. . . .

And that is how we destroyed the peace of rural England.

# XX

## TRAVEL TALK

ONE of the dangers of the League of Nations is that it may help to make the world one place and so make travel an easy and commonplace thing. The war had at least one good effect in making travel difficult again. It is no longer possible to go about the world unchallenged. You set out as a suspect, and, if you are not a habitual criminal already, the lady who takes your photograph for the passport transforms you into one. In the circumstances, you are a little surprised that George Nathaniel, Marquess Curzon of Kedleston, Earl of Kedleston, Viscount Scarsdale, Baron Ravensdale, Knight of the Most Holy Order of the Garter—who is not six persons, but one person—consents to make out your passport without demanding a personal interview. There is a good deal to be said for the old aristocracy, however. A marquess does not inquire too carefully into the print of your thumb. Even the Swiss Consul does not ask to

see your thumb-print, though he is extremely inquisitive about other things. He is not content
to give you the run of Switzerland, as the Italian
Consul gives you the run of Italy, on the word
of a marquess. He will visé your passport only
if you tell him the exact spot in Switzerland at
which you mean to get out of the train first, and
he gives you but three months' right of travel
compared to the Italian twelve. Considering the
photograph, however, it is impossible to blame
him. He is obviously taking a risk in admitting
so criminal-looking an alien into the country at
all.

But even now your trials are not at an end.
As you show your ticket at Victoria, you are
given a post card to fill in, containing all sorts of
questions comparable to "Who is your favourite
female character in fiction?" and "Which is the
virtue you most generally detest?" You are
warned that you will not even be allowed to go
on to the boat at Newhaven till you have
answered these, and you settle down to write out
the answers, when a little middle-aged man with
a thick neck opens the door of your compartment
and asks if there is room. He ought to know
that a railway compartment is a place in which
there is never any room, even when there is
only one person in it. The person or persons in

possession justly resent the intrusion of all new-
comers. He is probably aware of this, for he
mutters something about "men who have fought
in the war" in a truculent manner. It is impossible to tell whether he is boasting of having
fought in the war himself or blaming the rest of
us for having done so. He sits down, brings
out a morning paper of an inferior kind, folds
and slaps it in halves, folds and slaps it again
in quarters, folds and slaps it in eighths, and
begins to read it. He has not read a paragraph
when he begins to feel the heat, takes off his
bowler hat, stands up and carefully puts it in
the rack. He resumes his reading, but he has
not reached the end of the second paragraph
when he becomes aware of a trickle of cold air
on his thinning temples, lays down the paper,
stands up, reaches for his bowler and puts it on
again with an air of defiance. He then takes
out a notebook, turns over the pages, and jots
down a figure here and there till his head becomes hot again, when he rises and puts his hat
carefully back in the rack. In short, he behaves
exactly like a madman or a foreigner. Englishmen often do when they are in a railway train.
The traveller can no longer expect to see men
whose heads do grow beneath their shoulder, but
he still sees queer creatures enough—men, for

instance, who take off their boots in railway carriages and change without a blush into carpet-slippers.

Seeing that persons of this type are so much given to travelling, we can hardly be surprised that travellers are passed through a sieve at the frontier of every civilised country before being allowed to pass. It is rather annoying to be passed slowly through the sieve, and to have to submit one's case in a queue to the tired little man at the counter who examines the passports. Luckily, he seems to have a due reverence for the Marquess of Curzon, and he scarcely takes the trouble to examine the photograph of one who has so majestic a sponsor. He studies more closely the passports given by the lowlier Foreign Offices of Europe. He compares the photograph with the person whom it is alleged to represent, darting a suspicious eye in search of a false beard. One is not surprised, seeing that most foreigners look more or less like Bolshevists. We know from experience that there are many foreigners of irreproachable character, but it is beyond dispute that many of them have the air of being capable of anything from motor-banditry to a revolution. That is probably why an Englishman on his travels regards it as perfectly natural that the examination of his pass-

port should be a mere formality, while the examination of the passports of foreigners should be
conducted in the spirit of the prosecution of
Landru. He does not trust these foreigners any
more than the passport-officer does. His only
cause of worry is that he should even formally
have to take his place in a line of such suspects,
and that he should be continually having to write
out a short *Who's Who* account of himself,
merely because aliens have to be kept under observation. He does resent this indeed: he resents
having to show his passport and to wait for his
luggage to be examined. He hates a frontier
as a lion hates a cage, and all these barriers of
dull-looking and omnipotent officials exasperate
him as though he were being subjected to wrong-
ful arrest. He behaves very well in the circumstances: luckily, he is not eloquent in proportion
to his feelings about a world largely populated
by aliens.

That there are still Britons who look on a
journey to France or Italy as a rather risky
venture among aliens of doubtful character I
discovered the other day in Paris, where three
of us had got into a train bound for Modane.
Suddenly a tall young Scotsman, as lean as a
pole, with a scraggy red beard, put his head
round the corner and said: "Is there room here?"

He threw a tremendously heavy bag into the rack, and sat down exhausted. "I tipped the guard to put me into an empty carriage," he explained, "and I had hardly sat down when he let in three of the fattest women that ever lived. I daren't stay in the same carriage with them," he laughed nervously, "I simply daren't." He became talkative, and described how he had arrived in Paris that day for the first time in his life. He wanted to know how we—there were three of us—had reached the Gare de Lyons. He himself had come on the Underground from the Gare du Nord. We told him that we had come in a taxi. He opened his eyes in surprise, then shook his head knowingly. "Catch me trusting myself in a taxi in Paris!" he said. He has evidently a vision of himself being carried off to the Bois de Boulogne and stripped of his last sixpence. He was very inquisitive as to the ways of foreigners, and brought out of his pocket two little paper-backed volumes, one of them called *All You Need to Know in France,* and the other *All You Need to Know in Italy.* He dipped into them every now and then in the intervals of talking, and would then look up and tell us about his sister in Scotland, who appeared to have been a stricter Sabbatarian than he altogether liked.

By good fortune, nervous though he was, he turned out to be a consummate liar. As the train was not due to leave for another half-hour my two friends went off to get something to eat, enjoining us to let no one else into the carriage while they were away. I am ashamed to confess that I bear a distant resemblance to George Washington, and when tired men and women stumble up the steps of a half-emtpy railway carriage in an overcrowded train and ask if all the seats are taken, I can hardly help letting out the truth. The Scotsman, though he scarcely knew the French for twopence, told as many lies during the next fifteen minutes as if it had been his language from birth. He did it partly by signs and partly by making sounds that no one could possibly understand. He pointed at empty seats, counting imaginary occupants. He held up his fingers and proved mathematically that there were already at least ten places reserved in the carriage. An excited, stout woman would cross-question him in Italian; he would smile wistfully and count his fingers for her one by one. An angry Frenchman would point to one of the empty places as though to prove that it must be empty; the Scotsman would point to it with twice the Frenchman's energy in proof that it was full. Every time he had got rid of a group of foreign-

ers in this way he would whinny with delight and
tell me of something similar that had once happened to his Sabbatarian sister. At last I could
endure it no longer. I acquiesced in the man's
wickedness and hoped to benefit by it later on,
but I was heartily ashamed to be even a silent
partner in such an orgy of lying. I told him to
be sure to keep my place, and slipped out on to
the platform. I walked up and down, looking
in at the window occasionally to see him still
counting his fingers to suspicious ladies, still
pointing to empty seats, still moving his lips in
sounds that he thought he had learned out of
*All You Need to Know in France.* I never realised before that it is possible to tell lies so
efficiently in a language one does not understand.
It was all very deplorable, but no one else got
into the carriage. Each of us had a corner seat
through the night all the way to Modane. It
is an ill wind that blows nobody good.

How little French he knew I discovered at
Modane. when we changed into the train for
Italy. He made a really magnificent effort not
to tip the porter who brought his bag from the
Customs examination to the train. The porter
tried him both in French and in Italian, and at
last, with a groan, begged someone to interpret
him. "I didn't ask him to carry my bag," pro-

tested the Scotsman, when he heard what was
expected of him; "It's quite a light bag. I could
have carried it myself." People of all nationali-
ties urged him to pay up, but he declared in a
high voice: "It's ridiculous. I tell you it's a light
bag that anybody could carry." At last he asked
the porter how much he wanted, and somebody
said that a franc would do. He brought out some
copper coins and fingered two of them hopefully.
The porter made a face. We explained that the
value of the two coins together was an English
halfpenny. Slowly he counted out some more
amid a Bable of advice from the rest of the passengers, and the porter, with a look of disgust,
grabbed a handful of them and hurried away.
"How much did I give him?" asked the Scotsman. "About fourpence," I told him. He
cackled aloud. "The man's a fool," he said; "if
he hadn't been in such a hurry, I meant to give
him sixpence. Serves him right for being such
a fool!" Though he laughed, however, he was
still hectic with excitement after his long tussle
with the Customs and his struggle with the porter. He began to tell an uncomprehending Italian how stupid it all was. "There are far too few
—*troh poo*—men to examine all that luggage—
that *bagage*," he said. "There were only *dooze
hommy*—two men, you know—looking after the

whole lot. There ought to have been at least
*sayze,* or even *weet.* It's far too much for *dooze.*
The whole arrangement seems to me stupid—
*tray* stupid. *Pongsey-voo?"* He talked like that
for about an hour. The Italian, coming of a
polite race, nodded at intervals, and said, "Ah!"
or *"Oui, oui."* At last, tired of getting no response in kind, the Scotsman took out his little
book, *All You Need to Know in Italy,* and
settled down to the mastery of yet another
language.

As I watched his lips moving over his lesson,
I realised that, after all, the world is still as
full of curious figures as it was in the days of
Sir John Mandeville, and that the world of the
traveller is still as incredibly fantastic as it was
a thousand years ago.

## XXI

## PEERING INTO THE FUTURE

MAN is a pathetic creature who does not know what is going to happen even in the next five minutes. If you had been at the Goodwood races you would have seen thousands of people who would have given anything to know what was going to happen in the next two minutes. But the future is dark to them, even when they are so close to it that they seem almost to be touching it. To read the future, a man would need to have an eye in the back of his head. For the Greeks were right in calling the future the time behind us and the past the time before us. We who are less logical talk as if the future were something that lay stretched before us like a landscape—something into which we are marching with keen and comprehending eyes. Alas, we can march into it only backwards, and all that confronts our eyes is the long winding road of the past. If statesmen could see the future with

anything but the backs of their heads, does anyone think that history would have been such a
record of bumps and misdirections and fallings
into the ditch? "Look where you are going,"
people are constantly saying to each other. But
that is the very direction in which it is impossible
to look. The eyeless condition of the back of
the head is an eternal fact which governs all the
activities of statesmen. It may be that in time
we shall evolve a new eye where it is most needed,
or be able to invent a substitute for an eye. Till
this happens, the human race must inevitably go
on in the old ludicrous fashion, making the old
mistakes in politics, in love, and in backing
horses.

If human beings do ever succeed in developing
this third eye, it will, I think, be due most of all
to the exertions of betting men. No other class
of the community makes anything like the same
effort to see out of the back of the head. The
betting man fixes his occiput on the future with
a persistent optimism that would do credit to an
idealist. He feels that if only he concentrates
the back of his head sufficiently he may yet be
able to read the future clearly enough to make
himself a fortune. He also loves reading the
sporting Press in which journalists tell what
they, for their part, have been able to read with

the backs of their heads. Experience should
have told him that it is a little difficult to read
in that situation. But, like the climbers of
Mount Everest, he does not allow the word
"impossible" a place in his vocabulary. And
so when he reads that "Pharmacie should about
win" or that "Strathleven is now at her best
and can race out every yard of the distance,"
or that "Morning Light holds a palpably sound
chance," or that "we cannot ignore the chances
of Black Gown," or that "Whatever beats
Weathervane will win," or that "Tête-à-Tête
is a distinct danger," or that "Blackland is
greatly fancied by those in the know," or that
"Stingo at 6 st. 10 lb. is so lightly weighted that
his chances cannot be lightly dismissed," or that
"the shadow of Proconsul looms up all the
while," he feels as profoundly impressed as
though he were consulting the Delphic oracle.
He will never admit that the problem of reading
the future is an insoluble one. He feels that
somehow it could be done, and, if a clairvoyante
foretold three winners in succession, she would
rapidly make her fortune out of people who back
horses. But apparently the clairvoyantes seldom
commit themselves to anything so exact as a
racing tip. They prefer to give their clients
vague hints about meeting a dark man or getting

a letter or crossing the water, and their prophe-
cies, being vague, quite frequently come true.
But the clairvoyante can give us none of the hard
facts that we most wish to know. Even the
people who tell our fortunes with cards have no
magic by which they can tell us in advance what
will win the Goodwood Stewards' Cup. They
can prophesy an illness, but they cannot say
whether it is going to be elephantiasis or a tooth-
ache. They map out the future in amazing detail, but they always leave out the really essential
detail. It is all very well to tell a woman that she
is going to marry a dark man, but what she wants
to know is which dark man. It is as though what
the fortune-tellers told us were written in a
foreign language of which the most important
words were unintelligible.

Yet the belief that the future can be read is
no mere passing whim of the superstitious. It
is one of the ancient beliefs of the world. Even
those who objected to the soothsayers for peering
into the future, objected to them most vehemently because they regarded them as capable of
doing it effectively. They punished the soothsayer because they believed that he got his news
of the future from the Devil and would probably
use it for devilish ends. They did not laugh
at him, as many people laugh at him nowadays;

they were heartily afraid of him—so afraid of
him that they sometimes killed him. The general
public, on the other hand, usually preferred a
soothsayer to a genuine prophet, and, if they
had to stone either of them to death, it was more
likely to be the prophet. The prophet could
not be trusted to make to-morrow pleasant, and
the only reason for wishing to know anything
about to-morrow is that we wish to hear how
pleasant it is going to be. If we want to be
gloomy, we can always read history or look
around us. There is no need to call in the special
genius of the prophet in order to hear depressing
things. That is why, if you are a public man, it
is always well to talk about the future with a
rosy optimism. Do not tell Englishmen that
England is going to the dogs. They will only
dislike you for it. Tell them that, though there
are clouds on the horizon, you can already see the
sun bursting its way through them and flushing
the peaks of your native mountains. Tell them,
in other words, that " it will all be right on the
night." If you do, you will be a far greater
success than Elijah ever was, and, instead of
being fed sparingly by ravens, you will be fed
lavishly by gulls. There have been few great
successes among men who took a gloomy view
about the future. An occasional gloomy proph-

ecy does no harm; it even increases the pleasure
with which people hear the cheerful things you
prophesy afterwards.   But no one could tolerate
a Mrs. Gummidge who, instead of thinking of
the old 'un, moaned and groaned all the time
about somebody who was not even born yet.
Even the most skilled prophet will make himself
unpopular if he persists in telling people about
misfortunes about which they would otherwise
not have needed to trouble till they actually happened.   It is a good rule to look on the bright
side of things, especially if you do not know what
the things are going to be.

That is why one respects the tipsters who are
to be found on the race-courses haranguing the
crowds of simple people who have come to make
money on horses.   The tipster always tells you
that he has a perfectly delightful future in his
hand, and that you can have it for a shilling.   He
tells you that, if you have sense, you will go home
a rich man.   And that is about all that most
people want to know about the future.   There
are crises in life when other thoughts are upper-
most, but, as a general rule, the most comfortable
thing you could tell a human being is that he
will in a short time have plenty of money.
"Listen to me," says the tipster, "and I'll make
you more money on this one race than you could

make by working for a week." It is so pleasant
a future he foretells that you begin to think that
he may be able to read the future after all. That
is how he makes his money. He has to persuade
you by some means or other that he has an eye
in the back of his head, while you have not, and
he does this by conjuring up a beautiful mirage
of to-morrow and persuading you that it is the
real thing. It is a form of witchcraft, but the
witchcraft consists in putting a spell on you, not
in wringing its secrets from the morrow. For a
tipster on the race-course knows as little about
the future as Dean Inge. He succeeds because he
gives you the future you want, but he gives it
to you in the present, when it is of no use to you.

It would be absurd, of course, to pretend that
we can know nothing at all about the future.
We can make inferences from the past and present, and arrive at many a shrewd guess even
about the winner of a horse-race. But can we
ever be quite so sure about the future as the
tipsters would like us to believe it is possible to
be? In Monday's sporting papers, for instance, a
tipster had an advertisement, part of which ran:

### AT GOODWOOD, TO-MORROW,

I have news of

### A SURE WINNER,

and I want every reader of these lines to be on what I Know to be a really Safe Investment.

Only One, remember, for I do not delude you by sending two or three or four horses, or two for one race, or any such business——

JUST <u>ONE</u>, AND A <u>WINNER</u>!

And that is what you want, is it not?

You can make Certain of a glorious Goodwood if you secure this winner, for, whatever you may be doing, or thinking of doing, you simply Must be on this wonderful winner, for you can collect enough on this One to cover all your operations for the week, for it will be at a very fine price.

"What I know," the tipster added, "convinces me that this horse is a CERTAINTY." That, it seems to me, is a strong statement to make about anything so subject to chance as the ordinary horse-race. Many a man has impoverished himself by backing certainties, and book-making survives as a prosperous business largely because so many people persuade themselves that they are backing certainties when they are only backing horses. Betting, which is an amusing pastime, becomes an occupation for fools when it involves the assumption that we can know the result of a race in advance. The Greek word for prophet was "mantis," meaning "one who raved." Listening to the tipsters on a racecourse, we realise how excellent a description it is. For a tipster is only a prophet in little, and his ravings are as frenzied as those of any prophet who ever foretold the end of the world. And they are about as accurate. It is more economical and as sensible, when backing horses, to consult the stars. It may be that the news of the winners of the next Cambridgeshire and Cæsarewitch are written somewhere in the night sky, but, if so, they are written in a language that none of us can read. Hence it is well to be a little careless in your betting—to engage in it in the spirit of a game of guesses instead of bursting the back of your head in the frenzied attempt to see out of it. After all, if we could all see into the future, it would put an end to betting, and then what would there be left in the papers to read? So, perhaps, we are none the worse for the absence of that wonderful third eye.

## XXII

## THE SORROWS OF FREE LOVE

JEZEBEL has never been a popular character. Not even that last great scene in which Jehu is coming to kill her, "and she painted her face, and tired her head, and looked out of the window," has won the affections of anybody outside those circles, which are enthusiastic for all kinds of sinners from Absalom to the foolish virgins. It is true, as the *Encyclopædia* reminds us, that "what is told of her comes from sources under the influence of a strong religious bias." Even so, it is told so well that for most of us she remains immortally the incarnation of wickedness. Churchgoers for centuries have listened to the story of her murder without compunction. Jehu, they have little doubt, did well. "And he lifted up his face to the window and said, 'Who is on my side? Who?' And there looked out to him two or three eunuchs. And he said, 'Throw her down.' So they threw her down; and some

of her blood was sprinkled on the wall, and on the
horses; and he trod her under foot." And no
clergyman has ever reproved him. To the ultra-
Protestant mob Jezebel remained for generations
a prophetic figure of the Catholicism they hated.
They saw in Mary Queen of Scots simply the
repetition of her infamy, and in *Esmond* it was
"Jezebel" that the crowd shouted at the painted
old Catholic lady. We may one of these days
have a book written to prove that Jezebel was
as domestic as Queen Anne, but we shall no more
believe in a white-washed Jezebel than in a white-
washed Richard III. The condition of the world
can be explained only on the assumption that a
great many devils have lived in it. He-devils
and she-devils—people even worse than ourselves.

An odd thing about Jezebel is that, though
her main wickedness was not at all sexual, she
holds her place in the Puritan imagination as the
most scarlet of scarlet women. It is an interesting example of the Puritan habit of reducing all
sins to terms of the flesh. Jezebel's chief sin,
like that of Catherine the Great, was ruthless
Imperialism. As a character in the popular imagination, however, she is first and foremost a
painted lady. Faustina is another lady who has
come down to us with an inexplicably bad repu-

tation. Scholars in vain protest that she bore
Marcus Aurelius eleven children, that he
mourned and honoured her after her death, that
schools for orphan girls were piously founded in
her memory, and that there is no evidence against
her but gossip. The world will not lightly give
up its painted ladies. Is it not the painted ladies
who have brought about half the tragedies of
history? And the poets are as determined as
the public in this matter. In vain will scholars
protest that the Trojan War was fought for
economic reasons. To the common man it will
always be a war about Helen. Helen, however,
has been fortunate beyond most women of the
past with a past. She was sufficiently wise to
repent. As she calls herself a "dog" and heaps
reproaches on herself, she disarms the criticism
of the moralists as she did that of the Trojans.
Nothing could be more magnificent than the
charity of the Trojan old men when, seeing her
beauty as she came to them on the tower, they
declared that it was small blame that the Trojans
and the Greeks should make war for a woman
of such marvellous beauty. And even Priam said
to her in noble gentleness: "I hold thee not to
blame." In the stories of Helen, Cleopatra,
Iseult and Francesca, it is as though all censure
were burnt up in the fires of tragedy. Apart

from this, none of these women, except Cleopatra, could, save by a stretch of the imagination,
be described as a painted lady. The other three
might be described as monogamists at heart, who
happened to be married to the wrong men. They
were fastidious, not promiscuous in their passion.
They were faithful in their infidelity. At present, as anyone who reads the papers can see, the
world is enjoying a surfeit of painted ladies. In
the Divorce Court there have been a number of
sensational cases in which the chief actors seem
to have no distinguishing characteristic beyond
a general infidelity. We get the impression of
a riot of sex, a drunken orgy. There is no fas-
tidiousness, no choice, no continuity. There is
nothing but greed and confusion. Even Jezebel
had a purpose in life, but some of these lovers
have no purpose. Their very love is the result,
not of the urgency of a great passion, but of
indolent drift. They lust without imagination,
without taste. Many defences have been written
of Don Juan, but they have all been based on
the fact that he had imagination. Don Juan,
we are told, is the lover seeking the perfect
woman. He passes from one imperfect woman
to another in quest of his ideal. There is a sort
of noble fidelity in his pursuit, as in that of a
theologian who passes from creed to creed in

pursuit of the truth. Even if we accept this romantic interpretation of Don Juan, however—and we must be exceedingly innocent mystics if we can do so—it does not constitute a defence, but an indictment. There is no more foolish heresy than the chase after perfection among human beings. Belief in the perfectibility of man or the perfection of woman is, for all practical purposes, as wild an illusion as that of the man who climbed an apple-tree in order to lay hands on the moon. Men can live sanely only on the understanding that they cannot pluck the moon like an apple. They have to come to terms with their limitations and imperfections. The quest of the moon has to be condemned because it is unworkable. Most of the advocates of free love have been hunters of the moon. They have been youths, Rousseauists and Utopians. There is a period of youth in which the marriage tie seems an offence. The picture it conjures up of human beings tied to each other against their will, the idealistic boy regards as a parody of love. He holds—and in this he is reasonable enough—that it is the love and not the ceremony that is sacred. His chivalry is especially insistent that no woman should be bound for life to a man against her will. He dreams of perfect liberty for women. His theory of free love is at this time unselfish. In his enthusiasm, he is inclined to see in every woman who leaves a husband for a lover a human being rightly struggling to be free. When the wife in the play defends herself with the sentence, "All the purity that God has made cannot be bounded in a ring of gold," he applauds with flushed cheeks. He is violently Shelleyan and anti-husband. It is true that, on such occasions as he happens to be in love himself, he is entirely monogamous in his faith. He believes that he loves for eternity—that neither Heaven nor Hell could separate him from his love. He is a Bayard in his devotion, and lives in a state, not of theory, but of ecstasy. So soon as he ceases to be in love, however, he begins to theorise again. He becomes a philosopher in the intervals of love. He may be either a philosopher of enthusiasm or a philosopher of regret— possibly he may be both. If enthusiasm predominates, he will once more set to spinning Utopias in which men and women innocent as angels live in obedience to love. Having himself ceased to love, he realises that love may pass. Hence his angels have liberty to leave one another when they will. He does not like to think of them as growing into elderly or commonplace householders. He almost persuades himself that in an ideal world all life could be lived in the mood of the balcony scene in *Romeo and Juliet,* save that, when love grows cold, another balcony must be found. The philosopher of regret is more of a realist. He sentimentalises over the brevity of beautiful things, and falls back sympathetically on Horace's *carpe diem.* He believes in taking what pleasures one can. He resigns himself to a life in which beauty is rare but prettiness is abundant. He believes that a temporary refuge from dullness and drabness can be found in the garden of Epicurus. He sees the wise man as a connoisseur of flowers.

Those who theorise about free love may be for the most part Utopians. Those who practise it are almost without exception Epicureans. There are a number of mystical free lovers who stand half-way between these positions, such as George Sand, of whom it was said: "In George Sand, when a woman wishes to change her lover, God is always there to facilitate the transfer." Women are probably given to a greater extent than men to calling down a divine blessing on concupiscence. The majority of practising free lovers are less theoretical in their experiments. They are simply restless people seeking rest in change. They try to satisfy themselves with love without affection, with pleasure without fidelity. It is because affection and fidelity play

so small a part in their lives that they are for
the most part unhappy. One seldom reads the
report of a case in the Divorce Court that suggests that any of the participants have ever
enjoyed themselves. Love in them seems to be
merely an expensive form of gloom. They are
as unenviable as Madame Bovary. To compare
them to the moth in the flame of the candle
would be to flatter them. They have not even
the instinct of ecstatic self-destruction. They
live rather as the beetles on the floor. This is
obviously not true of all the men and women
who go through the Divorce Court. In the
Divorce Court are also to be found averagely
good men and women and more than averagely
good men and women. But there have been
various cases in recent months in which the men
and women seem to have tasted nothing of
pleasure but the dregs and heel-taps. They apparently know as little of happiness as stray cats.
They find love only in the refuse-buckets. Puri-
tanism, no doubt, has its faults, but it at least
gives love a home. It realises that without continuity and fidelity there is neither depth nor
dignity in love. We need not pretend that there
have not been exceptions to this as to all other
rules. But it is a remarkable fact that all other
great stories of illicit love are stories dignified

either by great suffering or by great fidelity. They are not stories of gloomy pleasure-seeking, but of ruinous destiny. In all of them the lovers are bound by chains as inseparable as the chains of marriage. There is no love without chains. Free love is a contradiction in terms. If it is free, it is not love; if it is love, it is not free. I have no doubt this has already been said by somebody else. He was perfectly right.

## XXIII

## YOUTH

MEN used to wish to be immortal. They do so in some countries still. When Professor Steinbach, of Vienna, announced that he had discovered a means of making old men young again with the help of monkey glands, he had five thousand telegrams of inquiry from Berlin alone within twenty-four hours. The depths of pessimism to which people have descended in England may be estimated by the fact that, when Mr. Albert Wilson announced that he had taken the gland treatment and become twenty years younger in consequence, and that he would lecture about it in the Albert Hall, only half-a-dozen people arrived outside the hall to hear the lecture. It must have been a pathetic spectacle. It would be interesting to know what their ages were and what they looked like. Were they six bald, toothless old men, helping along their ossi-

fied old bodies with the aid of sticks, squeaking,
doddering, rheumy-eyed?  And did they gather
there with a vision of the youth that had been
buried in each of them gloriously resurrected,
and sending the thrill of young blood rolling
through the pipes of their arteries and the hair
sprouting from their long-barren skulls like
young corn?  Whoever they were, they were
doomed not to learn the secret of growing young
again, for it appeared that Mr. Wilson, having
grown young too suddenly, had suddenly died
of the effort.  What was their mood when they
read the announcement on the door?  Did they
begin to reflect once more that if only they had
their lives to live over again they would make
a better thing of them?  Before reading the announcement of Mr. Wilson's death each of them
was possibly dreaming of living the old life over
again—of becoming once more "one of the bo-
hoys"—of seeing the West End of London by
night, of wine and paint and pleasure and police
courts.  But, so soon as the prospect of becoming
young again began to recede, I have no doubt
they began to imagine that they had intended to
live their second youth more wisely than the first
—to be a little more faithful and a little less vain,
to be a little more kind and a little less self-in-
dulgent—in short, to be good sons, good brothers,

good friends, good lovers, good husbands and all
the rest of it.  There is nothing more agreeable
than to live an ideal youth in retrospect.  One's
uncle always tells one, as he puffs at his pipe:
"Never smoke; if I had to begin all over again
—"  He tells one the same thing about alcohol
as he drinks his whisky-and-soda.  He attempts,
indeed, to lead the perfect life not in his own person but in the person of his nephews.  I understand that in the last twenty or thirty years a new
generation of uncles has arisen, and that the
modern uncle himself tries to behave like a
nephew and will scarcely admit the loss of his
youth while there is a tooth in his head.  But the
natural uncle—the uncle that has existed in all
ages except this—is a person who deceives himself into the belief that, if only he were young
again, he would be a model to his nephews.

On the whole, however, it is doubtful whether
the average man's desire to grow young again,
if he does desire to grow young again, is due
to any moral reasons.  We long for youth chiefly
because we like being alive, and youth, rather
than any later age, is the extreme opposite of
death.  But there is a limit to our desire to
be young.  How many men of seventy are there
who would submit to an operation as a result
of which they would dwindle and dwindle until

they were once more babies in the cradle, and
had to go through all the stages of life again?
How many would even consent to be sent back
to an infants' school or, for that matter, to a
boys' school? To be an undergraduate again—
that is another matter, though to submit to professors would seem an odious slavery. But the
undergraduate is, on the whole, at a stage where
there is a reasonable amount of freedom and
just the right amount of responsibility. Even
so, it is not every old man who would take back
the irresponsibility of youth at the cost of giving
up the long-acquired habit of dominating others.
That, indeed, is the special charm of the monkey-
gland treatment. It is not something miraculous
that transforms an old man into a boy; it leaves
one an old man in every important respect while
giving one back one's youthful energy. Hence
its appeal to the old. It has apparently every
possible advantage except that it kills you. We
must wait, however, to hear what happens to the
other old men who have been inoculated with the
glands of monkeys and goats. How, for instance, is the American gentleman of seventy-one
feeling who told an interviewer last August after
the operation: "I feel twenty-five years younger.
I'm a new man, full of 'pep,' strong, healthy, and
ready to go on with my work. I was ill, old and

played out, but the operation has revivified me"? How is the South African farmer feeling who called on a Transvaal surgeon a few months ago, leading a baboon on a chain, and in regard to whom we were told: "The doctor shot the baboon at the door of the operating-room, removed its gland and inoculated Mr. —— with it"? We were told at the time that the farmer had regained his failing sight and was, as a result, able to read without glasses. Poor Mr. Wilson in the same way began to grow hair again and to learn German in order to be able to converse with the lady to whom he had proposed. And now, in the flower of his youth, he has withered without warning, and the old-fashioned doctors are pronouncing his epitaph. They say that senile rats have been restored to youth by the gland treatment, and that they, too, begin to grow hair again, become spry and active, and then suddenly collapse. For myself, I confess I am prejudiced from the outset against a cure which seems to ally us with no animal higher than the monkey, the goat and the rat. I see a warning peeping out of the eyes of those dubious animals. To be a goatish old man or to be a man-monkey at the age of eighty is no great result from an *elixir vitæ*. I should prefer to trust my old age to sour milk or to the endless chewings of Mr. Fletcher.

Mr. Fletcher, I remember reading, was an old man at forty, abandoned by all the doctors, when he discovered that it was possible to chew one's way back into youth. Twenty years later he was turning somersaults at the age of sixty. He set people chewing all over the civilised world, and conversation disappeared from many dinner-tables. One of the greatest of modern novelists became notorious for his scowl when anyone spoke to him while he was counting his chews. He ceased altogether to observe human nature, and his brain did no work but registering numbers—"a hundred and eighty-one, a hundred and eighty-two"—until, just as he was about to swallow, "five hundred and sixty-five, five hundred and sixty-six, five hundred and sixty-seven." Whether he prolonged his life in this way it is difficult to say, and whether it is worth going on living merely in order to go on chewing is another question that is difficult to answer.

At the same time, all these attempts to find some way of living longer prove that at least some people think it a good thing merely to be alive. Very few people know why they wish to remain alive, but nearly everyone does wish it. Not that we take advantage of the amenities of this charming world while we are in it. We are content even never to go round it to see what

it looks like. We have invented a number of
abstracts words—Truth, Beauty, Love—but we
are not curious as to what they mean as we
are curious about the winner of the next Derby.
We regard Truth and Beauty as affairs for experts, and turn aside from them in search of
amusement. We prefer to live the lives of the
higher animals. The problem of how to keep our
hair from falling out costs us far more anxious
thought than the problem of how to make the
League of Nations a real thing. We show none
of that seriousness that the old preachers used to
urge on us. We are content to breathe, to satisfy
a number of our appetites, to amuse ourselves,
to share our amusements and our troubles with
others, to have a good night's sleep, and to be
able to do all these things without getting into
debt. We enjoy occasionally reading some great
man's utterance on "the dedicated life." There
is some chord in our being that responds to it.
But there is another part of our nature, that is
suspicious of ideals and that flies from them, as
a young girl flies from a bore. On the whole,
we believe simply in keeping alive and in helping
other people to keep alive. That is why any
man can always create a sensation by announcing
that he has discovered a means of prolonging
life or delaying old age. Most of us would be

glad to live till a hundred if we could be sure
of preserving our strength and our wits. There
are many people to-day who say they have no
wish for extreme old age in this world or for
immortality in another. The normal man, I
fancy, would like both. He does not, as I have
said, want to live for any reason in particular,
but he wants to live. He wants to be able to
run upstairs without feeling it—to eat and drink
what he likes without feeling it—to read the
cricket results without glasses—to cultivate his
garden—to play with his children—to enjoy
every hour of the day like a game. He prefers
this, indeed, to the life of an angel. He seriously
believes, indeed, that compared to his own life
in a suburban villa the lives of the angels are
insipid. He will accept immortality as something better than no life at all. But he cannot
imagine that Paradise has anything so entirely
satisfying to offer as a day at Lord's. Heaven
is a place without a City page, without a Sports
page, without a Sunday newspaper—perhaps
without a newspaper at all. It is a place in
which, according to the Salvationist hymn, "there
are no more public-houses," and it is doubtful
if there is a golf-course or even a card-table.
That is why some old gentlemen turn longingly
to the gland treatment. It does not offer to set

them dangling in a mid-air immortality, but to leave them in this charming Zoological Gardens of a world behind the bars of which they have grown accustomed to eat, drink and be merry.

# XXIV

## THINGS THAT INTEREST

MRS. BARNETT has some cause for complaint. She lectured for an hour on the necessity of improving the conditions of slum children and of saving thousands of them from an environment of crime, immorality and ignorance. It is a subject that makes a strong appeal to the heart and imagination. Yet the newspapers reported the lecture as though it had been, not a plea for poor children, but a vehement attack on the nursery rhyme, *Hey, Diddle Diddle, the Cat and the Fiddle*. Mrs. Barnett naturally protests. She evidently thinks the newspapers ought to have known better. And yet the appalling fact remains that her passing allusion to *Hey, Diddle Diddle* was to nine persons out of ten one of the most supremely interesting things she could have said. She cannot at least have said anything else that was more novel. She may have said true things, profound things, but to de-

nounce *Hey, Diddle Diddle* was an original act
that was bound to cause a general stir of excitement. We may call human beings silly and
trivial for allowing themselves to be distracted
in this way by the latest novelty. But novelty
makes us all gossips, and there are few men so
philosophic that they would not lay down the
*Phaedo* itself and look out of the window if they
knew that the Lord Mayor of London was about
to walk up the street on stilts and with a painted
face like a clown. Even the passion for truth
does not quite destroy the taste for novelty. A
new dance, a new song, a new fashion, a new
theory, will set the chins of the wise as well as
of the foolish wagging. Even philosophies themselves are interesting to the majority of people
only while they are novelties. The philosopher
becomes for a few years as popular as a dancing
dog: at the end of the boom, even the greatest
of them must take his place among the ignored
immortals. Everything tends ultimately to sink
into the condition of being taken for granted.
The great truths have to be re-created as novelties for each new generation. Otherwise they
will lie neglected under the dust of use and wont.
Hence, even great writers and great preachers
have to make concessions to the universal passion for novelty. To make old things new is a

part of their genius. Many writers, no doubt, make use of novelty, not as an advertisement of truth or beauty, but as an advertisement of themselves. They had rather be notorious than artists. There was one poet of our time who did his best to create a sensation at a dinner by casually eating the tulips out of a bowl in the centre of the table. As the other guests were too good-mannered to let it appear that they noticed anything unusual, the poet in desperation seized the bowl in both hands and swallowed a large mouthful of the water in which the flowers had been kept. Admittedly, the way of poets is hard, and it is no easy matter to make poetry interesting to an average human being. The poet with the tulips succeeded at least in making himself, if not his verses, memorable.

There is no doubt that it is becoming in an ever greater degree the tendency of newspapers to pay attention to poets who eat tulips. They will even give you a photograph of the poet sitting beside the bowl, which will probably be marked with a little cross of identification. They believe that news is only another name for novelties, and a man may nowadays become world-famous by saying that he saved himself from consumption by eating pigs' ears with a silver fork. Many old-fashioned persons believe

that this is an entirely modern form of silliness,
but, as a matter of fact, it was always novelties
that set human beings talking.  Even among
the most primitive peasants, the birth of a three-
legged foal causes vastly more excitement than
the birth of a four-legged foal, and a crowing
hen will be talked about throughout a country-
side to which crowing cocks are commonplaces.
The startling and the strange make the most
obvious appeal alike to the barbarous and the
civilised.  The ancient Athenians were, on this
point, at one with the savages of the South Seas.
None of us can escape the attraction of the
exceptional.  We welcome almost any break in
the monotony of things, and a man has only to
murder a series of wives in a new way to become
known to millions of people who have never
heard of Homer.  The other day there were an-
nouncements of many weddings in the papers,
but few of them were of the slighest interest to
anybody except the bride and bridegroom and
their tiny circle.  One of them, however, became
a matter of world-wide interest because the
bridegroom, in stepping aside to dodge an old
shoe, fell and bit his tongue almost in halves.
"Bridegroom Bites Off His Tongue," ran the
daily paper heading of the story.  Who would
pass it by without reading it?  No novelist dare

invent so ghastly an accident. No dramatist
dare do so, even for the Grand Guignol. At
least, one hopes he dare not. Yet, simply because
the thing had never happened before, it was
worth hurrying the tidings from America
through the bowels of the sea to all parts of the
world. Our appetite for news of this kind has
nothing cruel about it. It is simply the appetite
for the novel and the monstrous. The tastes of
human beings are exceedingly simple. They do
not care whether you are the fattest man on earth
or the leanest man on earth, whether you are extremely bald or extremely hairy, whether you say
an amazingly wise thing or an amazingly foolish
one. All that they ask is that, if you can, you
should be, do or say something that is superlative
of its kind and so out of the common. They are
collectors of curiosities, and their curiosities in-
clude men of genius and murderers, clever
cricketers and clever forgers, sages and buffoons,
spendthrifts and misers, winners of the Dunmow
flitch and co-respondents, the world's best verse
and the world's worst verse. In its rage for the
curious the human race is hardly more disturbed
by ethical considerations than a collector of
stamps. It seeks after the odd and the rare,
as a stamp collector seeks after certain three-
cornered stamps. If nearly all stamps were

triangular, the passion of the collector would
soon become quadrilateral.

If this were the last word to be said about
curiosity it would be a bad look-out for the
human intelligence. It would mean that most of
us see life as an incoherent museum of curiosities,
and there would be no public for any but the
*Tit-Bits* sort of paper. Luckily, there is nothing
that palls on us more quickly than curiosities.
Reason is the enemy of incoherence, and compels
us to look for meanings and connections in things.
The entomologist, rapturous as he becomes over
the discovery of a butterfly that has slightly different markings from all other butterflies, misses
the most lasting excitement of his hobby, unless
he ultimately discovers some sort of pattern running through insect life. The stamp collector,
in the same way, will in the end reduce his treasures to pattern and order. Literature dare not
attempt to dispense with pattern as a popular
Sunday newspaper may. The man of letters is
the man who in his writing satisfies our sense of
pattern. One of the chief differences between
Plutarch and the anonymous ladies who write
books of gossip, is that Plutarch gives us a
pattern of anecdotes, while the anonymous ladies
give us merely a jumble of anecdotes. Even
the most trivial gossip may become literature

if it satisfies our sense of the pattern in life, as
we may see in *Pepys's Diary* or the *Memoirs* of
St. Simon. There are two sorts of curiosity—
the momentary and the permanent. The momentary is concerned with the odd appearance
on the surface of things. The permanent is
attracted by the amazing and consecutive life
that flows on beneath the surface of things.
Inconsecutiveness, which begins by interesting,
ends by wearying, us. Even a newspaper would
suffer in circulation if it appealed only to our
love of the inconsecutive. Its readers demand
of it some kind of consecutiveness of pattern
and policy, whether in its attitude to politics or
to life, or to the choice or arrangement of the
news. It is difficult to say how far the average
human being can be trusted to prefer the consecutive to the inconsecutive. That he does so
to some extent, however, is suggested by the
fact that there is no daily edition of *Tit-Bits*.
And, even in his interest in Mrs. Barnett's attack
on nursery rhymes, it may well be that the
average newspaper reader did not stop short at
enjoying a novel monstrosity of opinion. He
was puzzled by the philosophic challenge of Mrs.
Barnett's views. His theory of life included the
acceptance of the necessity of a great deal of
play and nonsense for children and of a little

even for grown-up people. He took it for granted that some brightness of colour might be brought even into the slums by those nonsensical nursery rhymes, which are almost the only poetry he knows. He could not imagine a happy nursery without nursery rhymes, or happy nursery rhymes in which the cow did not jump over the moon. Thus, he was horrified by what Mrs. Barnett had said, as by a devastating and revolutionary doctrine. If what Mrs. Barnett said was true, then his whole theory of life was wrong, and there was nothing left for him but to bring up his children in the blind alleys of reason. Luckily, he does not believe that what Mrs. Barnett said was true. He is content to regard it as the pardonable error and heresy of a noble mind. The old nursery rhyme has come through the ordeal unscathed. Meanwhile, we must at least be grateful to Mrs. Barnett for entertaining us with the most startling literary opinion that has been uttered since the death of Samuel Butler.

# XXV

## BEGGARS

THERE never were so many beggars in London. At least, not within living memory. And the worst of it is, they have none of the romance of beggary. They are prosaic, dull, hopeless. Most of them look as if they had been born to be commonplace citizens, earning a more or less honest living. To speak strictly, indeed, they are not beggars, but collectors. They stand on the kerb; they wait in the doorways of restaurants; they haunt the streets of the respectable. All the time they keep shaking their narrow white boxes, rattling the coppers that the charitable have given them and asking for more. They vary from the sullen to the responsive. Some of them seem to demand a right rather than to beg a favour. They believe that there is money somewhere, and that it is only just that it should be shared. It is the habit of civilised societies, at the end of a great war, to provide kerbs fit

for heroes to stand on.  Heroes are no longer
so willing as they used to be to accept this as
a fitting reward.  Even so, heroes, like other
human beings, are strangely submissive.  To be
licensed to beg is better than to be allowed to
starve.  And so the West End of London, which
a few years ago used to be alive with the tinkle
of sovereigns, is at present alive with the dull
clatter of pennies in wooden boxes.  Strangers
to town are at first depressed by the spectacle.
Their hearts are touched.  They begin by giving
to everybody.  They feel a boundless charity
that flows out in copper and at times even turns
into silver.  Every beggar they see is a new
man.  They pity him personally.  They shrink
from the sin of passing by on the other side.
After a week or so they begin to give here and
to give there, but cease to give everywhere.  If
they have given at the door of the restaurant,
they can refuse on the kerb with a good conscience.  And if they have given on the kerb,
they feel justified in not seeing the man with the
box at the entrance to the Underground.  As a
matter of fact, they have become a little impatient of such an incessant appeal to their
charity.  At first they pitied every beggar as a
man wronged by society—wronged almost by
themselves.  Now they begin to feel as though

it were they themselves who were the aggrieved persons. They are not sure that other people, however poor, have a right to annoy them so persistently. They can hardly walk down the quietest street without being interrupted by a man with a money-box. What they object to most of all, perhaps, is that it puts them in a false position. They cannot refuse without appearing niggardly, and, as they have to refuse sometimes, they are aware of the beginnings of a feeling of hostility against men who make them look niggardly. By the end of a few more weeks they have ceased to see the average collector as a human being in whom they have any interest. They think of him, if they think of him at all, more and more as a nuisance. They probably take little more notice of him than a reader takes of the recurring commas on a page. If they do, it is because he is a comma misplaced. He has lost his original significance. They may still on occasion see him imaginatively, but it is only on occasion. Their charity is no longer constant, but spasmodic.

I do not think the thin black line of beggars fits in well with the London landscape. In Italy it is different. Beggars seem to be a natural part of Italy. They are picturesque in decay. They have crooked hands that are fit for nothing else.

Their thanks are musical—*"Grazie, signor!"*
They are a race by themselves, living in the
shadows of church doors. They have a long tradition of poverty, and have adapted themselves
courteously to a life of dependence on the passers-by. The Italians are a charitable people, and
it is said to be they and not the foreign visitors
who keep the beggars in bread. English and
American visitors are apt to take it for granted
that any man can earn enough to keep him if he
is willing to work, and to resent the sight of men
who voluntarily choose a life of idleness. I am
inclined to doubt the theory that any man can
earn a living if he pleases. Almost any man of
strong character may, but the man of average
character is a creature of circumstances. Luckily
for the beggars, the Italian does not ask whether
a man is fit to work, but what he wants. And
the average beggar wants so little that to be
charitable is one of the cheapest of hobbies. The
Italian climate, on the other hand, is more suit-
able to begging than the English. For the
greater part of the year it is warm enough to sit
idly at a church door without discomfort. In
England idleness during at least half the year
is misery. There have never been any English
beggars of the romantic kind except tramps, who
warmed their blood with walking. There are few

to-day except gipsies, and even the gipsies have
become little more than a nuisance. In London,
at least, the beggar is a mere figure of wretched-
ness. Most pitiful of all are the blind who sit
reading the Scriptures with their fingers, or who
clasp a handful of match-boxes and wait for the
sound of the penny dropped into the tin cup
hung round their necks. Hardly less wretched
are the old grey-haired women who sit under the
arches of bridges with a tray of match-boxes and
studs and such pretence of merchandise. They
are blown upon by every wind, especially by the
cold wind from the east that finds its way round
corners. To sit in the wind and the dust, as
they do, for a single day would give an ordinary
respectable citizen his death of pneumonia. I
have heard it maintained that these wretched
creatures do not feel the cold, and that there is
no need to waste pity on them. This is too comforting a belief. The beggar under the arches,
no doubt, survives as the soldier in the flooded
trenches did; but it is not through want of sensi-
bility. Happier, much happier, the beggar who
can warm himself by singing! And yet, strange
to say, it is the itinerant musician who of all
beggars wins most of our sympathy. He sings
songs that we do not wish to hear; he plays airs
we dislike on an instrument that we detest. But

he appeals to us somehow as a decayed artist.
He may blow his beery breath under a beery
nose into a cornet that can emit only discordant
blasts of pain.  But he is in his way an artist,
and, at anyrate, it is better that he should go
and drink more beer than that he should go on
playing the cornet.  The man with the hurdy-
gurdy and the man who goes round with a gramophone do not attract us in the same degree.
They are beggars disguised as artists—hawkers
of ready-made and imitation music.  How different is the flute-player or the fiddler!  Here are
artists, and artists even with noble instruments.
They live in the finest tradition of beggardom.
They play to please us, not merely to annoy us
into paying them to go away.  There was an
admirable old man in Dublin who played the
flute in the streets right down to the coming of
the Black-and-Tans.  When he played it outside
a fashionable hotel, he played *God Save the
King,* because he knew that the people in the
hotel would like that.  When he played it in a
poor street, he played *The Soldiers' Song,* because he knew that the people in the poor street
would like that.  Could courtesy go further?

As for beggars in general, one's attitude to
them is curiously paradoxical.  One's heart is
often fullest of sympathy for them on the very

days on which one will not go to the trouble
of giving them a penny. It is almost entirely
a matter of weather. If it is a cold day, one
feels so distressed at the spectacle of a poor
man that one would go to almost any lengths
in order to help him. As it is a cold day, however, one is closely wrapped up, and the notion
of undoing all one's coat-buttons and glove-
buttons for the purpose of giving a fellow-crea-
ture so trivial a sum as a penny seems positively
ludicrous. It would be making a mountain out
of a mole-hill. Besides, it would be making a
public exhibition of charity. One likes to bestow
the copper sort of charity hurriedly, stealthily,
unseen of the passers-by. On a fine, sunny day
one can do this quite easily. One is unimpeded
by an overcoat. One can transfer a penny from
a pocket to a blind man's tin almost by sleight
of hand. But, alas, it is so warm that one takes
it for granted that everybody, like oneself, is
fairly happy. There is an old story of a farmer's
wife who, on seeing a beggar coming to the door
on a bitterly cold day, said to her servant: "Mary,
go and give that poor old woman a bowl of hot
soup." The farmer's wife herself felt so cold that
she went into another room, took out the brandy-
bottle and helped herself to a glass. She felt its
generous warmth spreading through her frame.

She then went back to the kitchen. "Mary," she said, "you needn't bother about that bowl of soup. It's not so cold as it was." It is a cruel story, but, really, when one thinks of one's own behaviour, one does not feel like throwing stones at the farmer's wife.

The best rule is probably to give a penny to anyone who looks as if he were asking for it, whether it is wet or fine. It may seem an easy thing to do, but as a matter of fact it is almost a counsel of perfection. One can do it on a holiday, for giving money to beggars is a natural part of a holiday. But it is extraordinarily difficult to keep it up. Either you take a sudden dislike to some particular beggar, or you see somebody else giving him money, and you feel, "Oh, well, that's all right." I have never been able to feel charitable, for instance, to those beggars who attempt to sell you large earthenware pots of ferns when you are walking along the street. One of them particularly I detest. He comes up beside you, and says in a husky voice: "Do you want to be my friend? Do you want to be my friend?" And he does not stay for an answer, but attempts to thrust the pot into your arms. It is only a pretence. He has had the pot for years. It is his disguise. It enables him to pass for a merchant.

But I cannot take a sentimental view of beggars. I do not like them. I wish they were abolished. Their poverty, it seems to me, is a crime. And it is our crime rather than theirs. That is why I think that it ought to be suppressed.

## XXVI

## THE LAST OF THE STREET CRIES

ONE of the compensations for living in London in August is that we occasionally hear the voice of a man or woman crying lavender through the streets. Lavender is the only thing that is sold as all beautiful things ought to be sold. It is sold to a song: every other ware is sold either to a shout or in silence. The muffin-man in his white garment has, I fancy, disappeared with his bell for ever. He, too, brought music into mean streets, even for those of us who shrank from eating his muffins. The milkman, happily, is left as a relic of old times, going around with his hand-cart and crying "Mi' O!" like a strange cat as he approaches our doors. The dustman also still utters a shout as he bangs on our side door for admittance, but it is merely a noise like the inarticulate yell of a man in a nightmare and bears no resemblance to the "Dust O!" of the noble fellows who once drove their treasures of

rubbish to Boffin's Bower. Not that I suppose
the dustman to have ever been so picturesque
a figure as he appears in a certain print described
in one of Mr. John Ashton's books. He is there
displayed with a very clean face and "attired in
a yellow jacket, green waistcoat, crimson knee-
breeches, blue ribbed stockings, and brown
gaiters." At the present day, in his sou'-wester
of sacking, he is the drabbest of shapes as he
lobs down the path with a silver bin on his back.
Silver, I say, in obstinate refusal to face the
fact of the ugly bucket-colour of my dust-bin.
We cannot grant the dustman a clean face, as
the old illustrator did, but we can at least invent
for him a pretty appurtenance. I confess to a
preference for the itinerant knife-grinder, with
his queer spindle-legged paraphernalia of wheels,
straps and round stone to set the teeth on edge.
He does not, in crying his trade, use either words
or music, and the only knife I ever gave him to
sharpen he certainly returned blunter than it
was before he had sharpened it; but I feel none
the less tenderly towards him on that account as
a seedy relic of the world of travelling tradesmen
that preceded the present world of stores. The
coal-heaver in his lovely corduroy waistcoat used
to make a fine uproar as he announced his journey through the streets. He may do so even now

in some places. For my part, I never perceive
him in these days save as a silent figure sitting
lonely on his bags and gazing out at the world
with a black face and bloodshot eyes. Would
he might shout! I cannot help wishing, too, for
the return of the cockle-seller leaning sideways
with a heavy basket on his or her arm and shouting for customers. There was never a more inarticulate shout. As a child I often tried to
translate it into speech, but I never got nearer
it than "Awpie! awpie! awpie!" In those days
even water was sold in the streets from carts
shaped like prostrate barrels, and the water-
seller would bring it to the door in a great
wooden bucket. I remember, too, the man in
white who sold honeycombs, which he carried on
a plate on the top of his head, a skilled balancer.
It was impossible to stay away from the window
when he was passing. He seemed eight feet
high, and his voice was full of sweetness. But
that is all long ago. The old order has changed,
giving place to the new. And the lavender-
seller is left, a mere sign and memory, like a
shell on a mountain-top, recalling the days when
a sea of wonderful things covered the world.

I heard a man crying lavender yesterday. The
plaintive melody he sang compelled me as ever
to go to the window. I am sure the Highland

reaper sang nothing more likely to make one
stop and listen.  It is a whine, a beggar's appeal,
transmitted and made beautiful.  London becomes a summer day at the sound.  If ever a
tune had a dying fall, and affected one

> like the sweet south
> That breathes upon a bank of violets,
> Stealing and giving odour,

it is the song of the lavender-sellers.  What
the words of the song are I am not quite certain.
It begins, I believe:

> Will you buy my sweet lavender,
> Sixteen branches for a penny?

But other verses are sometimes sung, commend-
ing it as a plant full of virtue against the moth.
For myself, even in this year in which moths
flutter through the air like petals in a June
orchard, I cannot bring myself to associate the
song with utility.  To regard a song of this
sweetness as the music of disinfection would be
unpardonable.  My own attitude to the song is
purely voluptuous.  If I give a penny to the
lavender-seller, it is not in return for lavender,
but in return for the song.  It brings to the

imagination a trim, old and orderly world, a
world in which every house has a garden, and
men and women grow flowers instead of potatoes.  I know a man who says that the street cry
of the lavender-seller always depresses him because it reminds him that the end of the summer
is approaching.  Most of us would as soon think
of being depressed by the spectacle of silk butterflies speeding on their light lumbering way above
the hollyhocks.  All frail and lovely things cause
us a pang when we think of them as a part of
the procession and chorus of mortality.  But it is
the departure of life, not the departure of summer, that is our grief.

The man I saw peddling lavender yesterday
was a sturdy middle-sized beggar in a tumble-
down hat and a weather-beaten coat.  He had
a face of brick, with anxious wrinkles about his
eyes.  He had beyond question a good voice for
shouting coke.  Every time he sang he stopped
in his walk, put his hand up to one side of his
mouth like an Irish ballad-singer, and howled
till the blood came into his forehead.  It was
impossible to distinguish the words, but the music
was recognisable, and, if it had not been, there
were the long, dried-up, purple rods in his hand
to reveal his purpose.  I confess I found the
ugliness neither of his voice nor of his colour an

offence. His trade made up for everything—his trade and the song he sang so badly. He was as charming as Horace Walpole. He bound one to the world of one hundred and two hundred years ago, when life was not a business but a picture. At least one likes to think so. It is not only sentimentalists who are drawn in their imaginations to old customs, old jingles, old phrases, old houses, old dress, old paintings, even old pronunciation. There is no one more fortunate than the man for whom a long train of yesterdays comes alive at a word, at a sound, at a glimpse of a snuff-box or a tapestry or an old wooden cradle. How delightful it is when tradition, instead of hiding away with a printed label on it in the chill of a museum, appears in the streets as a hawker's cry or a Regency house or a cross-timbered public-house with mediæval angles! If one loves the lavender-seller for one reason more than another, it is that, even when he is at his hoarsest and shabbiest, he informs the working world with the presence of an elder city. It is difficult to understand how the voice of a single hawker or a single bird should suddenly make the whole air populous with invisible life up to the very sky when it had been empty and dull a moment before. But who is there who has not experienced this miracle?

Will you buy my sweet lavender,
Sixteen branches for a penny?

One never hears this but one seems to follow
the notes as they die away into the reaches of
infinity. Usually it is a woman who sings it.
She adds the tragic appeal of a begging woman
to the appeal, already sufficiently exquisite, of
her song. . . .

But the chief reason why I, at least, like to
hear the hawkers crying lavender is probably
different from all this. It is simply that lavender
used to grow outside the door of a white-washed
cottier-house on the top of a hill where I once
desired to live as indifferent to the day's news
as Thoreau. If London Pride had grown there
instead, I should have loved London Pride, and
have argued against those who despise it and
say that it is ugly. As it is, the scent of lavender
has always for me the faint scent of an ideal
never accomplished or even attempted. Who
is there who would not rejoice to be reminded
of the days when Thoreau and Emerson came
into the imagination like sons of the morning
and filled him with the longing to be at once a
loafer and a god?

## XXVII

## WILD LIFE IN LONDON

WILD life may be studied in many parts of London. Perhaps the most interesting place of all is a law court, in which a wild animal, disguised as a tame animal, sits at a desk and takes measures to keep other wild animals in order. On the whole, however, the study of man as a wild animal does not make for happiness. The more closely we observe the antics of man as an animal, the more depressed we become. Had Swift studied weasels instead of men, he would never have written *The Voyage to the Houyhnhnms*. Had Anatole France studied penguins instead of men, he would never have written *Penguin Island*. It is a curious fact that all the men who write about rats and foxes and spiders are cheerful, while all the men who write about the animal called man are sad. Man is disgusting when he is thought of as an animal. Ways that would amuse us in a dog or a field-mouse we regard as degrading in a human being. We cannot forgive

man even that element of rapacity which he
shares with most of the wild animals. To follow
instinct, which is their exquisite duty, is in him
a revolting crime. We do not allow him to be
as greedy as a pig, as venemous as a serpent, as
cunning as a fox, as savage as a wolf, as cruel as
a cat, as lecherous as a goat, or as irresponsible
as a cuckoo without a protest. He is capable, if
we can trust the reports in the papers, of being
all these things, but no one defends him as
naturalists will lovingly defend the cat and the
cuckoo. There were novelists who called themselves naturalists in the nineteenth century, but
they lacked the great essential of naturalism—a
settled cheerfulness in presence of the animals
they study. One felt that they positively hated
man. The spectacle of his ordinary life reduced
them to the deepest gloom. Walt Whitman said
many bold words on behalf of man the animal,
but all the while he was secretly idealising man
as an unconquerable spirit. The poets, indeed,
in their inspired moments, write almost without
reference to the animal in man, and none of the
great lines in poetry describes him at his food or
performing any other of those functions in the
performance of which he is as the beasts that
perish. We, too, may reasonably do our best on
occasion to forget the animal of whose greed and

cruelty we read in the Sunday papers. If we
are fond of animals, there are more charming
animals to be seen even in the heart of London.
Have not the sea-gulls already come back to the
Serpentine for their winter holiday?

The most attractive animal I have seen in
London was a duck. I was standing on the edge
of the Round Pond in Kensington Gardens. It
was one of those blowy days on which the Round
Pond is a tumultuous ocean, whipped by the
storm into huge rollers six inches high. As the
little model yachts ploughed their way across the
pond, many of them heeled over till their main-
sails dipped into the tide. Two of them had their
sails so heavily weighted with water that they
were unable to right themselves and lay helpless
and drifting on their sides. Had I been the
owner of a model yacht, I should have been timid
of racing in such foaming seas. The English
are a race of seamen, however, and, even with
the spectacle of the wreckage spread out before
them as a warning, the yachtsmen loosed their
green and their blue and their white boats into
the wind as though they had not a fear. There
are no other yacht races to compare in excitement
with those on the Round Pond. Cowes is dull
compared to it. Each race takes exactly the
right time—two or three minutes—and the spec-

tators can follow it from start to finish. But it was not in appreciation of yacht-racing that I began to write. Man is a spirit, not an animal, in battling with circumstances such as wind and tide. Nor do animals organise games in this serious fashion. The animal that delighted me, as I have said, was a duck. Superficially, it was like all the other ducks on the pond. If all the ducks in Kensington Gardens were marshalled before me for purposes of identification, I could not pick this one out. Yet there must have been something different about it. The ordinary duck, when it sees a yacht bearing down on it, scuttles out of the way as human beings do when getting out of the way of a motor bus. Never but once have I seen a duck showing any interest in a yacht except for the purpose of not being run down by it. This duck, however, I repeat, was different. A beautiful green yacht with bellying white sails bore down on it while it was not looking, and the duck, on turning its head round after a vigorous preening of its breast feathers, suddenly beheld the deck leaning over towards it and almost touching its tail, as though inviting it to step aboard. Whether it was startled into its next action I do not know, but, quick as lightning, it wheeled round and, to the amazement of the assembled spectators, scrambled on

to the deck and took up its position at the tiller.
The yacht wobbled for a moment under the unexpected weight, but the duck wobbled too, and
so kept its place.  In so heavy a sea a heavy
duck was an advantage to the yacht, which no
longer lay over at a dangerous angle, but began
to move in stately speed across the pond.  For a
time the duck looked about it as though a little
puzzled by the motion and by the seascape that
swept past it at so incredible a speed.  If the
boat lurched under a sudden squall the duck
gave a frightened lurch also.  But, as it kept its
footing on its magnificently flat feet, its self-
confidence seemed to grow, and it gazed round
at the other ducks with an air even of boastfulness.  At last, as though to suggest that it had
been accustomed to sailing for years, it ceased
even to look round at the others and began to
nibble vigorously at its breast feathers like a
duck on dry land.  By the time the yacht was
drawing near the opposite shore the duck appeared to be settling down to sleep, but, on
looking up, it saw a crowd of men, women and
children laughing uproariously at it, whereupon
it slid hastily off into the water and floated off
towards the middle of the pond with a ruffled
air of contempt for so ill-mannered a race. . . .
That, I think, is the most exciting event that

has happened in Kensington Gardens in recent years. I am sure that no one who was present on that blue and billowy day and who saw the duck going for a sail will ever forget it.

But do not be excessively disappointed at having missed it. There are other excitements to be had by observers of wild life in Kensington Gardens. Are there not still a few squirrels left? The grey squirrel of London has many enemies. He is suspected as an alien of destructive propensities, and there were even rumours some time ago that orders had been sent out for his extermination. But the squirrels, like other aliens, survive persecution, and there are still two or three of them to be seen searching for acorns under the trees on these autumnal days. There are few prettier sights in London than a squirrel standing on its hind legs and nibbling at a nut that it holds between its forefeet. How swiftly its teeth set to work, as though it were apprehensive that an enemy might appear before it had had time to eat it! How it pauses now and then, the nut still held near its mouth, and looks and listens for a sign of danger! How jealously it greets another squirrel who comes and watches it at its feast! You would think that there must be acorns enough in Kensington Gardens, quite apart from the monkey-nuts that amiable ladies scatter, to satisfy the few squirrels that fly among the tree-tops. But squirrels, alas, are as the dogs that bark and bite, or as the cats that rush after one another up trees. One squirrel that I watched, at least, was not content to sit upon the ground and eat his nut quietly when another appeared round a tree-stem. He thrust his nut whole into his mouth and rushed at the other as though he would have murdered it. The latter fled up the tree, round and round the trunk, with the pursuer close on its tail. The squirrel with the nut paused at the first branch, sat in the angle of it, took the nut in its forepaws, and began hurriedly nibbling it again. The other, in the crook of a branch just above it, crouched like an angry cat, its tail curved along its body till it touched its ears, and uttered sounds that were half like a cat's mewing growl and half like the chur of a nesting partridge. It was as though every nibble the other took cost it a pang. How it wept! How it wailed! Never was sorrow like that squirrel's sorrow. After a time the squirrel with the nut became irritated by such plaintive accusations, took the nut between its teeth, and once more gave chase among the branches. At times it would pretend to give up the chase, turn backwards, and would pause, its head hanging towards the ground, and its limbs stretched out.

Then the complaints would begin again farther
up the tree, and the chase would be resumed, till
at last the second squirrel sprang like an acrobat
among the topmost leaves and set off on a journey from tree-top to tree-top, which is the squirrels' High Street, and so out of sight. Had
children behaved like this, I should have condemned them; but it was a pleasure to see
squirrels behaving so badly. And, to judge by
the crowd of people who paused under the tree
and smiled at the little lamenting squirrel, as its
sides shook with sobs, others enjoyed it as much
as I did. Who could condemn an animal with
such a panache of tail?

But neither the duck that went for a sail nor
the weeping squirrel filled me with quite the
same astonishment as did a little greenish-yellow
bird I saw in Hyde Park perched on a low bush
within a few yards of Rotten Row. It looked
a little melancholy, and was so wrapped up in
its melancholy that it seemed perfectly indifferent to the many people who halted to stare at so
curious an apparition. It was like no bird that
I had ever seen. At first I thought it might be
a canary of some strange breed that had escaped
from a cage. But it was no more like a canary
than like a yellow-hammer. It had a small,
round, rapacious hooked bill such as I had never

seen on a green or yellow bird before. There is only one bird that it resembles even in the pictures in the bird-books, and that is the serin. I shrink, however, from boasting that I have seen a serin in London, because the serin is an extremely rare bird even in rural England, and I know how offensive such boasts are to those who have been less fortunate. Besides, I did not really enjoy seeing the serin—or, rather, the bird that looked like a serin—half so much as I enjoyed seeing a willow-wren an hour later dancing silently from shoot to shoot in a clump of bushes on the edge of the Long Water in Kensington Gardens, its green fading in flight into the green of the leaves. How thoughtful of the loveliest of the birds to linger in town in the first week of October, when all wise willow-wrens have taken wing for the sunshine of the south! But even the willow-wren must not tempt me into boasting. It is better to be content to say, as anyone may say, "I have seen rooks in Rotten Row. I have seen bats over the Serpentine." For even these things, common though they are, never cease to delight. The rook, the bat and the sea-gull—how a dead city breaks into life at a mere movement of their wings!

**THE END**